W

The Revd Canon Rachel Stowe was
Central Prayer Correspondent
for the Mothers' Union from 1987–1992.
She is an honorary Canon of St Albans
Cathedral and lives in Pertenhall, Bedford.

WOMEN
at PRAYER

An anthology of prayers
by Mothers' Union members
from around the world

Edited by
The Revd Canon Rachel Stowe

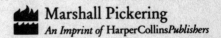 **Marshall Pickering**
An Imprint of HarperCollinsPublishers

26414

Marshall Pickering is an Imprint of
HarperCollins*Religious*
Part of HarperCollins*Publishers*
77–85 Fulham Palace Road, London W6 8JB

First published in Great Britain
in 1994 by Marshall Pickering

10 9 8 7 6 5 4 3 2 1

A catalogue record for this book is
available from the British Library

ISBN 0 551 02800-9

Typeset by Harper Phototypesetters Limited,
Northampton, England
Printed and bound in Great Britain by
HarperCollinsManufacturing Glasgow

Prayer
Reminds us
Abba Father
You are
Ever
Real

Pauline Beswick
Lichfield diocese, England

Contents

Preface

Prayer is, quite simply, communication with God. Talking to Him, listening to Him, just being with Him.

Is there a right way to pray? A worker at a church-run women's refuge went to call on a young woman with two small children who had returned home but was still in great fear of her violent and unstable husband. The worker went to the back door and was quickly ushered in to discover that the husband was battering the rather flimsy front door, threatening to knife his wife and children. The wife and the worker lay on the floor, thinking to shield the children if he did get in, knowing these could be their last moments on earth. But the police arrived in time and took the man away. Afterwards, over a very shaky cup of tea, the wife said to the worker, 'I wanted to pray but I didn't know the right words . . .'

In our everyday lives the right words are the ones which come straight from our hearts to our Father in heaven, who knows us and loves us as we are: happy, sad, guilty, afraid, rejoicing, confused, angry, reflective, full of energy or exhausted. These prayers have been written by ordinary women and girls in everyday situations and collected by Mothers' Union members from many parts of the world simply to help us all get closer to God, our Abba Father, who is forever real and ready to listen to us, whatever our circumstances. They can be used in whole or in part; the right words are your words. But do use them, for as the poet Tennyson said, 'more things are wrought by prayer than this world dreams of.'

Rachel Stowe

General Acknowledgements

My grateful thanks to all who have contributed towards this book, most of whom are Mothers' Union members from many different parts of the Anglican Communion. Right from its foundation by Mary Sumner in 1876, prayer has played a central part in the work of the Mothers' Union, and on admission members commit themselves to be regular in prayer, worship and Bible reading. As can be seen from the Wave of Prayer chart (see Appendix), Mothers' Union members in each Anglican diocese pray and are prayed for on a rota, the idea being that as each takes their turn a wave of prayer constantly circles the earth, so that at any moment there should be a branch, group or member praying. As four out of five members live outside the United Kingdom, and many do not have English as their first language, this wave of prayer encompasses a great diversity of languages and dialects.

Making a selection has been hard, and there were many more prayers I would have liked to include had there been space. I have tried to keep any editing to a minimum so that each prayer can speak directly from the situation from which it comes. This great variety has made the compilation of *Women at Prayer* a fascinating exercise. No matter what part of the world you come from, who cannot fail to be moved by or identify with the anguish of a mother whose son has gone astray, the continuing sadness caused by a stillbirth or miscarriage, the trauma of a marriage breakdown or the death of a loved one, the constant fear in war-torn countries or the hardship of the refugee camps? Or feel uplifted by all the joy and happiness as well: of the bride and groom on their wedding day; of delight at the beauty and complexity of God's creation; of the birth of a baby within the family or the neighbourhood; of deep awareness of the revitalizing power and peace of God the Father, Son and Holy Spirit?

Each day has been marked with the major festivals of the Church's year, a saint or other revered man or woman, taken from the calendars of many parts of the Anglican Communion, and whose biographical details can be found in appropriate reference books, or from the 1990 Calendar of Holy Women published by Peregrina Publishing Co. of Toronto M4P 2A8, Canada. This selection, for reasons of space, has to be arbitrary, but it is intended to give the assurance that whenever we pray we are surrounded by that marvellous great communion of saints, known and unknown, throughout the ages.

Especial thanks to Mothers' Union staff at Mary Sumner House, London, and in particular to Gill England and Alicia Little of the Publications department, and Janet Bailey of the Faith Development department for their help and expertise, especially in the complex and lengthy matter of trying to track down copyright; and to Barbara Lawes, chairman of the MU Overseas committee, for her invaluable worldwide contacts.

In addition to the many individuals, branches, dioceses and provinces in the Anglican Communion who have contributed I would also like to thank the Mothers' Union in the dioceses of Birmingham, Chelmsford, Chichester, Coventry, Edinburgh, Exeter, Gloucester, Llandaff, London, Manchester, Monmouth, Newcastle, Norwich, Oxford, Peterborough, Portsmouth, Rochester, St Albans, St Asaph, Salisbury, Southwark, Winchester, Worcester, York; the Province of Ireland and the UK Young Families' department; for permission to use prayers from their own publications and events. I am also grateful for permission to use prayers from *Joined in Love* by Rosemary Atkins, Dorothy Brooker, Rosalind Buddo, Philippa Chambers, Audrey England and Alice White of New Zealand; *A White Candle* by Mary Oakley and *Stepping Stones* by Maureen Sutton, both of England.

All efforts have been made to trace copyright ownership of selections included in this anthology and to obtain permission for their use. The publishers would appreciate notification of any inadvertent omission of copyright acknowledgement.

The peace of prayer

Step out of life for a moment,
out of the shout and the glare,
into that silent sanctuary,
into the peace of prayer.

Turn your back on the tumult,
let the world's din slow down,
forget the crowds and laughter,
forget life's ugly frown.

Stand in that still white hush,
that is flooded with light and peace,
where the soul can seek refreshment
and the body get release.

Tell Him the things that hound you,
tell Him the things you fear,
speak to Him of your troubles
for in prayer He is very near.

Tell Him the fight you're having
to keep your life set square,
tell Him the things that mean so much
that you feel you cannot bear.

Tell Him you're frightened of what's ahead,
that you wish you knew the end,
tell Him those things – for He alone
will help you as a friend.

Prayer is not only asking
for things that we badly need,
it's talking to one who understands,
one who will always heed.

One who will give us courage
to go on once again,
one who, however much we ask,
we never ask in vain.

Enid Lewis
Chelmsford diocese, England

JANUARY

New Beginnings

January 1st – NAMING OF JESUS
New Life

Father, in your Son you brought us new life.
So, in this new year we give our new beginning to you.
Grant us new life, new love, new dedication to your way,
that through the days to come we may, by your grace,
grow closer to you.

Rochester diocese, England

January 2nd – Mary Ward, religious 1585–1645
Prayer of an expectant mum

Lord God Almighty, the creator of our world and every
living thing upon it, how can I thank you for the
wonderful gift of a new life, growing within me now? No
praise is enough for the miracle that is happening to me. I
know that my baby is developing day by day, and from the
very tiniest beginnings is taking on the shape of the boy
or girl, man or woman who will become my son or
daughter.

Sometimes I find all this too much for me to imagine;
but I want to understand your will and your ways, O
Lord, and to thank you with my whole heart.

Accept my humble thanks and praise, for the sake of
your own Son, Jesus Christ, our Lord. Amen.

Joy Hawthorne, Manchester diocese, England

January 3rd – Gladys Aylward, missionary 1970
Beginning a meeting

Father, as we meet together help us to listen, to
understand and to remember. Make us aware that we are
meeting not simply with one another, but with you: make
your presence real to each one of us.

As we listen, help us to concentrate so that we really

hear what is intended, and what is your will.

Give us courage to say what needs to be said and humility to accept decisions with which we do not agree.

When we finish our meeting, enable us, by your grace, to go out and fulfil your purpose, doing what you want us to do; and to your name be the glory, through Jesus Christ, our Lord.

Mothers' Union Anthology of Public Prayers, United Kingdom

January 4th – Angela of Foligno, mystic c.1248–1309
Starting work again

I'm starting work again tomorrow after . . . . . years.
I'm excited God, but oh so scared!
I feel I'm out of date, but they did seem pleased to see me.
May I find fulfilment in this venturing out.
Lord God, help me to keep a right balance between family, home and work; help me to keep my priorities right so our home will continue to be a place of love and security.

Joined in Love, New Zealand

January 5th – Tallulla of Kildare, abbess 590
Sharing a new interest

We've never had time on our hands before Lord.
You know the busy lives we've had.
Now in our small house and tiny garden there's not nearly as much to do.
The grandchildren don't need us as often as they did.

So we offered to help at . . . . . last week. Was that your idea?
There wasn't a lot to do, sandwiches for me to spread and . . . . . drove the car to pick up some who can't drive any

more. We had a lovely day! We talked to people we knew and people we didn't.

He found some toys in the crèche that needed mending. That'll keep him happy for a month!

I'm sure we're going to enjoy our weekly turn down there. It's given us a new interest together and something fresh to talk about. Thank you, Lord, for leading us there.

Joined in Love, New Zealand

January 6th – Epiphany
Guided by a star

We read, Lord, of the Wise Men of the East who were guided to you by a star, and who brought generous gifts of gold, frankincense and myrrh. Give us the wisdom to seek you, light to guide us to you, courage to search until we find you, graciousness to worship you and generosity to lay great gifts before you, who are our King and our God for ever and ever.

Salisbury diocese, England

January 7th – Lucian, theologian and martyr 312
Leaving home for the first time

Heavenly Father, we ask you to bless . . . . . who, for the first time, is leaving home and family and friends. Help him/her to know your love and constant presence wherever he/she is, and protect him/her in mind and body. Fill him/her with the power and joy of your Holy Spirit and keep him/her faithful to your Son, Jesus Christ.

Mothers' Union Prayer Book, United Kingdom

January 8th – Pega of Croyland, mystic c.719
Birth of a new baby

Loving Master of all masters, Jesus Christ, we thank you
for the new-born babies in this world. Place your loving
hand into theirs so that they may grow well and
spiritually and know you fully.

   Four women from Kigezi diocese, Uganda

January 9th – Gregory of Nyssa, teacher c.394
New mothers

Lord Jesus, you know what it is like to be exhausted,
stretched to the limits and alone. We pray for all new
mothers. They can get so tired: too tired to bake, to iron,
to hoover, to shop; too tired even to think of you, to pray
or to go to church; everything can be all too much. Help
us to show that we care, that our society cares, and that
the Church cares. We pray that whenever an opportunity
arises we can show our care by our practical help.

   We ask you to help us share and care in your name and
for your sake.

   *Kate Smith, MU Anthology of Public Prayers, United
Kingdom*

*January 10th – William Laud, archbishop and martyr
1645*
A garment for a new baby

I haven't much to offer as I'm not very rich,
But God gave me a gift of love so I've put some in each
stitch.
So when you wrap it round your child with care and
tender love,
I pray that God will clothe your child forever in His love.
   Marjorie Andrews, Monmouth diocese, Wales

January 11th – Mary Slessor, missionary 1915
Prayer for midwives and nurses

Heavenly Father, we thank you for your love especially to women who work with poor people, teaching, nursing, and helping women during their labour. We pray you give them wisdom; guide them always to fulfil their duties without difficulties. Lord, be with those they work with and send your Holy Spirit to give us love to help all mankind. We pray you lead us through Christ, our Saviour.

Yunice Clement Bazia, Maridi diocese, Sudan

January 12th – Marguerite Bourgeoys, religious 1700
Created for a special purpose

Lord, I know you created me for a special purpose, to serve you in a unique way. You have given me a gift, and talents, a certain something no one else has. Help me to be a valuable link in the chain of humanity, help me to find peace and meaning in what I do, knowing no one else can be me. In Jesus' name. Amen.

Salisbury diocese, England

January 13th – Hilary of Poitiers, bishop and teacher 367
For children starting at a new school

O Lord our heavenly Father, we thank you that you have blessed us by giving us children. Through your guidance we have managed to bring them up to your standards.

May you be with them as they start their primary school. Let them love to learn and respond to whatever their teachers will teach them. As they approach their exams, let them be firm and steady and do what you will direct them to do.

Merciful Father, remain their personal Saviour as they

go to secondary school. At this age they are mature enough to make fruitful plans for their future. This is the time when they are anxious to know different things. May you give them a steady mind so that they do not fall into worldly dangers. Let them concentrate on their studies and guide them to choose good careers which will lead them to a bright future. For those who are weak in their studies, Lord let them not lose hope, but know that you have plans of welfare for them.

Our Father, to those going to boarding school be their light so that they are able to cope with the change. Give them love so that they are able to socialize with other children from different places. We pray that whatever they will do may be for the glory of your name, through Jesus Christ, our Lord.

Zeridah Sendegeya, Muhabura diocese, Uganda

January 14th – Sava, bishop and missionary 1235
Passing on our faith

Lord, you have given us a sacred trust to pass on our faith in you to our children and grandchildren. Give us, we pray, a gift from you that we may do so with firm conviction and gentle trust, believing that you will take our effort and use it for your glory. In Jesus' name we pray. Amen.

Maureen Sutton, Chester diocese, England

January 15th – Kentigen, bishop c.603
A grandmother's prayer

Christ be in them and around them; these children of our children, given to us for a time to love and cherish.
Christ be in us, that through us they may see Him and learn that He is in them.

J. Campbell; St Andrew's, Dunkeld and Dunblane diocese, Scotland

January 16th – First Franciscan martyrs
Open to new life

Lord, make me willing for change to happen in my life as it did for the first believers. May your Spirit fill my thoughts, fellowship, work and prayers today.

Peterborough diocese, England

January 17th – Antony, abbot 356
Moving to a new place

Lord, our everlasting God, we pray for our family members and relatives at large that you may grant us peace and mercy. We pray that we may find the new place safe. We pray that we may find this new place in a peaceful manner because in your presence everything is all right. We pray that we may not find terror in this place and that you may grant us courage, peace and strength to overcome Satan's temptations. We know your Son Jesus Christ overcame Satan; may our spirits be strong enough to overcome his temptations. We ask this in the name of the Father, the Son and the Holy Spirit.

Four women from Kigezi diocese, Uganda

January 18th – Margaret of Hungary, religious 1242–1270
Courage and wisdom all the year

O Lord of all little things, strengthen me with your
gentleness so that nothing small or mean can upset me. O
Lord of all great things, strengthen me with your power so
that no disaster can overcome me. Give me courage and
wisdom so that nothing can prevent me from doing your
will and walking in your ways this year, and all my days.

MU Prayer Book, United Kingdom

January 19th – Wulfstan, bishop 1095
The gift of a new day

Thank you, Lord, for a quiet night's sleep and the gift of
a new day. Protect and bring safely to evening all my loved
ones and those connected with them. May I harm no one
in thought, word or deed, and do my best to give help
when it is needed.

Thank you for all the help you have given me over the
years and may I be worthy of it. Through Jesus Christ,
our Lord.

St Asaph diocese, Wales

January 20th – Fabian, bishop and martyr 250
New task

Father, I have been asked to undertake something that I
have not done before. I feel unsure of my own capabilities.
I ask, 'Why me?' Help me to feel your presence near me,
to guide and encourage. Help me to know your will in
this and to use the gifts that you have given me.

Chelmsford diocese, England

January 21st – Agnes, martyr 304
True happiness

True happiness is to know I need you, Lord Jesus, and know you are there when I'm sad; to be humble like you, and want to be obedient.

True happiness is to forgive as you forgive me, and purified to see you Lord; to work for peace and to be called your child.

True happiness is to be persecuted for you, for obeying you and following you; to rejoice in my reward, being with you in heaven for ever.

Marjorie Hodbod, Blackburn diocese, England

January 22nd – First martyrs of Spain 304
New incumbent, priest or minister

Almighty God, our heavenly Father, whose Son, Jesus Christ, humbled himself to be the servant of all; give us grace that as . . . . . comes to lead us in our parish we may be guided by your Holy Spirit to work together in peace and harmony, so that our parish may be a beam of light to your glory and to the furtherance of your kingdom; through the example of our Lord and Saviour, Jesus Christ, who is our strength and hope now and for the days to come.

The Mothers' Union, Province of Ireland

January 23rd – Yona Kanamuzayi, deacon and martyr 1964
Sharing worldwide

O Lord our Father, creator of the whole earth, we thank you for the most precious gift of life. Help us to use our lives in loving and serving you and all our neighbours throughout the world.

Open our eyes and ears to catch the sounds and sights of people of differing lands and tongues, so that we shall grow to understand their joys and laughter, their problems and their pain.

Inspire us day by day to follow your Son's teaching, telling the Gospel in every land with minds and hearts and hands ever glad to share with one another the beauty and bounty of your world.

Betty Wright, Monmouth diocese, Wales

January 24th – Francis de Sales, teacher 1622
For women's groups

Dear Father, thank you for bringing women together, especially for the purpose of the Church. Keep all such groups warm in your love. Make them joyful in their worship of you. Teach them through scripture how to grow in your love and be edified by your grace.

Prepare each member to be a true witness to your word, salt and light in their communities; and make them willing to be used by you in the work of evangelism. In Jesus' name we pray.

Ebun Carr, Gambia diocese, The Gambia

January 25th – CONVERSION OF ST PAUL
Witness

Heavenly Father, we thank you that we have been chosen to be witnesses to our faith. The road was never easy for Jesus and the Apostles and it will not be easy for us. Help us to show our faith by example rather than by words which people cannot understand. When we meet with antagonism guide our thoughts and our tongues that we may in a simple way tell of your love for us and all who believe. In Jesus' name.

Vera Grant, Portsmouth diocese, England

January 26th – Timothy and Titus, companions of St Paul
Be with us Lord

Lord, when you seem far away, draw near to us; when we
are afraid, lighten our darkness; when we are down, lift
us up. This we ask in your dear name.
   Guildford diocese, England

January 27th – John Chrystostom, bishop and teacher 407
For speakers

We pray today for our speaker . . . . . and we ask you to
grant, O Lord, to all speakers the power of your Holy
Spirit to direct their speaking and to make them sensitive
to the needs of those who hear them. Strengthen them in
prayer, study and preparation; give them listening ears and
humble hearts and keep them from the love of popularity;
and help them to speak the truth with courage and
wisdom, so that their words may glorify your name.
   MU Service Book, United Kingdom

January 28th – Thomas Aquinas, teacher 1274
For teachers

Father, whose Son our Lord went about as a teacher, may
all who teach in our schools, colleges and universities be
inspired to teach with skill, imagination and impartiality,
guiding all students into a search for knowledge and
truth. Lord in your mercy, hear our prayer.
   Portsmouth diocese, England

January 29th – Charles Frederick Mackenzie, bishop 1862
New opportunities in retirement

Lord, as we go forward to retirement we thank you for the
blessing of past years. Help us to adjust to our different
lifestyle; to grasp the new opportunities given,

remembering the needs of others; to use our leisure creatively; and in the new-found joy of time together, may we continue in your love and service.

Margaret Wilson, MU Anthology of Public Prayers, United Kingdom

January 30th – Charles I, martyr 1649
Never alone

Help us Lord to know that you will never leave us to handle our problems alone. Help us to see how much you have done for us and to learn to worship and praise you. Help us Lord to see beyond the immediate difficulties and to pray to you for victory.

Janet Nyenda, East Ankole diocese, Uganda

January 31st – John Bosco, religious 1888
God's strength

Father, we thank you for the knowledge that though weak and helpless we are, you are strong and mighty. In your strength we can do all things. Direct our course, we pray, and give us the power to stop at no obstacle, but go through victoriously to your praise and glory. This we ask through Him who died that we might become your children – even Jesus Christ, our Lord.

Bo diocese, Sierra Leone

FEBRUARY

Growing Roots

February 1st – Bridget of Ireland, abbess c.525
Guiding children in the holy way

We are before you, Lord, asking you to be with us in the family. You were born of the Virgin Mary, you grew in a holy family full of love for all. We beseech you to guide our children in the holy way. Burn up in them all things that displease you and make them meet for your heavenly kingdom.

   Maranga Banda, Mzuzu diocese, Malawi

February 2nd – PRESENTATION OF CHRIST IN THE TEMPLE
Candlemas

Today Lord, let me light three candles in another life –
a candle of comfort,
a candle of hope,
a candle of courage.

   A White Candle, Bristol diocese, England

February 3rd – Saints and martyrs of Europe
Lighting a candle

O God our heavenly Father, as we light this candle and watch the flame grow, kindle within us afresh the flame of your Holy Spirit. Let us so glow with your love that others may see you in us and want to know you; in our homes, our Church, our parish, our diocese. Bless those who light candles each day as a token of witness to the light of your power and glory, and to the coming of your kingdom on earth. This we ask in the name of Jesus.

   St Asaph diocese, Wales

February 4th – Manche Masemola of Sekhukhuneland, martyr 1928

Lighting a candle at home

This flame reminds me to ask you, Father, to fill me with your Spirit. How else could I hope to live today as Jesus did? By the power of that same Spirit I pray for those people, some of whom I will meet today, who have a need of you but do not know the answer yet. I am willing for you to use me to share the knowledge of the love of Jesus. Please give me the sensitivity, the skill and the courage; in the name of Jesus.

St Asaph diocese, Wales

February 5th – Agatha, martyr 250

A prayer for our child's home

Dear Lord and Father, when you sent your Son Jesus Christ to live amongst us, you gave Him earthly parents to take care of Him and to bring Him up in a happy and loving home.

Help us to prepare a warm and peaceful home to welcome our child; teach us that it is not an abundance of worldly goods that will bring happiness, but that our constant love and patient care will surround our baby with all that is needed for his or her wellbeing.

Give us your gifts of patience and gentleness, of understanding, love and peace, so that we may bring up a happy and contented child. We ask this for Jesus' sake.

Joy Hawthorne, Manchester diocese, England

February 6th – Martyrs of Japan 1597
Thoughts on waking

God knows me,
God loves me,
God has a use for me today.
God use me.
  Salisbury diocese, England

February 7th – Colette, religious 1447
Getting pregnant

Almighty God, we thank you for the gift of children and
for the women who are pregnant. We pray you bless all
the pregnant women and we pray that you give them faith
and hope.

Give strength to those who are weak and especially
those who live in villages and far from ante-natal clinics.
Give wisdom to traditional birth attendants who care for
them; give them love and ability so that they are able to
help the pregnant women.

We pray all this through Jesus Christ, our Lord.
  Four women from Kigezi diocese, Uganda

February 8th – Jacoba da Settesoli, religious c.1273
Not getting pregnant

Almighty God, loving Father, we thank you that you
created men and women and that you bless them with the
gift of children. We pray, loving Father, for those women
who have failed and cannot get pregnant due to many
problems. We especially pray for them that you will bless
them with children, and let them sincerely trust in you
and know that life is not only having children. We pray
for their husbands so that they know your will and will
not mistreat their wives for childlessness. We pray for the

immediate members of their families that they may love them and not have negative attitudes. Most of all, our Father, give them faith and the gift of salvation. Through our Lord, Jesus Christ, we pray.

Four women from Kigezi diocese, Uganda

February 9th – *James Mata Dwane, priest 1916*
Not wanting to get pregnant

O God, we pray for the families who have got many children. Bless them so that they may be able to care for these, your gifts, Lord.

God, we pray for the mothers who don't want to get pregnant. Help them to realize the need to try and plan for their families and lives, so that they are able to get the right advice. Give the social workers love, courage and wisdom to be able to help those mothers.

We pray all this through Jesus Christ, our Lord and Saviour.

Four women from Kigezi diocese, Uganda

February 10th – *Scholastica c.547*
For new parents

Loving heavenly Father, who with each new day bestows the precious gift of life, we ask you to bless the homes of young children, and especially new parents . . . . . and . . . . ., that they may feel your strength and guidance in their new responsibilities.

Through your Son, Jesus Christ our Lord, child of a loving home.

The Mothers' Union, Province of Ireland

February 11th – Caedmon, poet c.680
Keep me serving

Father, give me love in my heart when my family needs me
to do things for them when I had planned to do something
for myself; when they all run off to do their thing and
leave me with the mess or chores undone. You know,
Father, how much I like to do my own thing. Help me to
have love in my heart when I am serving, so that through
serving my family, I can serve you, in Jesus' name.

Sheila Armstrong, Southwark diocese, England

February 12th – Ethelwold, bishop and abbot 984
Prayer for orphans

God our heavenly Father, Lord of peace, God of love, we
pray you guide all children who have lost their parents
and are living in hard times. Lead them in everything they
do, send your love into the hearts of those caring for
them. Let this group know your love for them and they
will praise you.

Penina Tito Bazia, Maridi diocese, Sudan

February 13th – Absalom Jones, priest 1818
An engaged couple

Lord, we are so much in love and spend so much time
thinking about each other. Help us not to be possessive,
but to keep our wide circle of friends. Help us to grow to
understand each other. Help our love not to blind us to
differences that we must accept in our own individual
uniqueness. We know we have to work at our relationship
but we are tempted to think that everything will just fall
into place and be wonderful. Help us to be open with
each other, and let others share our great happiness.

Chelmsford diocese, England

February 14th – Valentine, martyr 269
Those about to be married

Most blessed Father, from whom all pure love comes, bless all who are shortly to be joined together in marriage. Grant that the hopes and prayers in their hearts may be fulfilled through your mercy.

Draw them ever closer to one another and to you; give them grace to bear one another's burdens and to share one another's joys; and grant that they may live together in faithful love to their lives' end, through Jesus Christ, our Lord.

Nan Deedes, Winchester diocese, England

February 15th – Thomas Bray, missionary and priest 1730
Marriage — early days

Lord Jesus, when you were at the marriage feast you turned water into wine, and so we ask you to bless our marriage. As the months turn into years please help our love to increase so that we ride through troubles and joys together, holding close to each other and to you.

Rochester diocese, England

February 16th – Philippa Mareri
The gift of a daughter

Thank you, kind Father, for your gift of a daughter like mine. She has her own home and husband now and always welcomes us there with open arms and heart. She cares for and about people and shows this in many small ways with unexpected gifts of flowers and cards. She sparkles and laughs a lot but enjoys silence, and in her presence the world seems a better place. You know all this as you made her, but I want to voice my gratitude.

Rochester diocese, England

February 17th – Janani Luwum, archbishop and martyr 1977

For too many girls in one family

Lord, we are always very sad – come and strengthen us. As we stay with husbands and children we give our hearts to you. Lord, if it was because we sinned have mercy on us. We put this into your hands through Jesus Christ, our Lord.

Nora Kazaango, Yambio diocese, Sudan

February 18th – Martin Luther, priest and reformer 1546

For a parish/deanery/archdeaconry/diocesan Family Day

Dear God, our loving heavenly Father, whose Son Jesus Christ said 'Let the little children come to me', inspire the lives of all those sharing in this day through its fellowship and fun, and lead us to a deeper understanding of your love for all your children. Through Jesus Christ, our friend and Saviour.

Norwich diocese, England

February 19th – Philothei, abbess and martyr 1589

For children growing up

Lord Jesus, friend of little children, I thank you for what you do to make little children happy in their play, in their work at school and at home. I praise you for your love and glory. I ask that they are purified, enlightened and inspired as they grow in your light to serve in the community in which they find themselves. I pray you help them in your holiness and truth so that they can be useful citizens in service to their families and their nation.

Joanna Cofie, The Gambia diocese

February 20th – Mother Cecile Isherwood 1906
Help us

Our Father in heaven, we thank you for our children.
When they are happy, help us to share their happiness
with them;
when they are cross, help us to bring them back to
calmness and peace;
when they bring us their secrets, help us to listen with
respect and understanding;
when they seem to be far from us, help us to be wise and
patient;
and at all times help us to trust in you ourselves, that they
may see in us how much difference it makes to live close
to you.
This we ask in Jesus' name.

MU Young Families' department, United Kingdom

February 21st – Saints and martyrs of Africa
African's prayer

I have no other helper than you, no other father; I pray to
you. Only you can help me. My present misery is too
great. Despair grips me, and I am at my wit's end.

O Lord, creator, ruler of the world, Father, I thank you
that you have brought me through. How strong the pain
was – but you were stronger. How deep the fall was – but
you were deeper. How dark the night was – but you were
noon-day sun in it.

You are our father, our mother, our brother and our
friend.

Africa

February 22nd – Confession of Peter
For non-Christians in the family

Dear Lord and Father, please help the members of my family who do not seek your love. As you look after your family, please help me to look after mine, and help them to open their hearts and minds to you. I want to share my faith and joy, but they do not listen.

I ask this in the name of your Son, Jesus Christ, who died to save us all.

Joy Edwards, Monmouth diocese, Wales

February 23rd – Polycarp, martyr c.155
Forgive a worrier, Lord

I'm a worrier, Lord, forgive me.
I know you are with me and will guide and help me.
I can feel you with me when I'm happy and when I'm sad.
When I'm angry, resentful, frustrated – I know there's no need – and yet I go on – and I worry, Lord. Forgive me.

Gwyneth Carter, York diocese, England

February 24th – Vocation of Francis of Assisi
Playgroup helpers

Lord Jesus, who said 'Suffer little children to come to me', bless our playgroup and all who help in it. Give us patience and understanding; enthusiasm and zeal; a right understanding of true purpose in life. Bless the children committed to our care and grant that any success which we have may be for their good and to your glory.

London diocese, England

February 25th – Walberga, abbess c.779
For children's safety

Dear Lord, we pray earnestly for our children, as we strive to bring them up in a hostile world. We pray for their protection against evil men and women who would seek to harm them. We pray for their protection from the misleading freedom offered by drugs and alcohol.

May we not be afraid to speak out against evil, and give us the courage to challenge what is wrong in society.

Lord, we long for the day when our children may once more walk our streets without fear of abduction, attack or bomb threat. May we never neglect our own responsibilities to our children, and fill us with your Holy Spirit that we may be empowered to bring them up as children of the Light.

We ask this in your holy name.

Lynne Kind and Jean Warham, Lichfield diocese, England

February 26th – Photeine of Samaria 1st century
Growing together in love

Heavenly Father, we have committed ourselves in love to one another for better, for worse, for richer, for poorer, in sickness and in health.

We pray that throughout our lives together you will give us grace to be true and faithful to each other. Help us to consider, support and comfort one another in times of trouble; to be patient and forgive one another's mistakes; to grow together in love and understanding sustained by the vision of a lifelong relationship.

We pray that we may know the joy of your constant blessing and live together for your glory.

St Albans diocese, England

*February 27th – George Herbert, priest, pastor and poet
1633*
A grandmother's prayer

Lord, teach me to love my grandchildren as a
grandmother should: not interfering, only understanding;
not pushing myself, just being there when wanted. Teach
me to be the sort of grandmother my children and my
grandchildren would want me to be.

Chelmsford diocese, England

February 28th – Oswald of Worcester, archbishop 992
A mother's prayer

Dear Lord, I pray to you for all children, especially those
who face: examination stress, divided homes,
unemployment frustrations, drug addiction or just feeling
unloved.

Teach me to temper love with discipline and discipline
with love. Help me to listen, to love, and when the time is
right, to let go.

Strengthen me in times of difficulty and
disappointment, but keep me open always to the joy of
motherhood. For your dear name's sake.

Joan Rich, Perth diocese, Australia

MARCH

Signs of Active Growth

March 1st – David of Wales, bishop and missionary c.601
Witnessing

Lord of light – shine on us;
Lord of peace – dwell in us;
Lord of might – succour us;
Lord of love – enfold us;
Lord of wisdom – enlighten us.
Then, Lord, let us go out as your witnesses, in obedience
to your command; to share the Good News of your
mighty love for us in the gift of your Son, our Saviour,
Jesus Christ.
  Arglwydd,
Agor ein llygaid i'th ganfod di o'r newydd.
Agor ein meddyliau i ddysgu mwy amdanat.
Agor ein calonnau i'th garu yn fwy tanbaid,
Agor ein gwefusau i'th foli a gwneud dy Enw yn hysbys
yn ein Plwyfi,
yn yr Esgobaeth, yng Nghymru, ac ym mhob man.
  St Asaph diocese, Wales

March 2nd – Chad, bishop and missionary 672
Speakers

O God, our loving Father, whose Son, Jesus Christ spoke
to mankind through the parable; we ask your blessing on
those who have offered themselves as speakers. Enable
them to speak with confidence and clarity, so that those
who listen may be receptive to what they say.
  Through Jesus Christ, our Lord, who through the
scriptures still speaks to us today.
  The Mothers' Union, Province of Ireland

March 3rd – Cunegund, religious c.1033
Lent

As the days lengthen, and the earth spends longer in the
light of day, may we spend longer in the light of your
presence, O Lord. May the seeds of your word which have
been long buried within us grow like everything around us
into love for you and love for other people, a visible
declaration of your lordship in our lives.

Grant, Lord, that there may be a springtime in our lives
this Lent.

MU Anthology of Public Prayers, United Kingdom

March 4th – Women's World Day of Prayer
Prayer groups

Lord Jesus Christ, you have promised that when two or
three meet together in your name, you are there in the
midst of them. We pray for all who belong to prayer
groups. May your love fill their hearts and the light of
your presence guide their praying. Give them grace to
respond with gladness to your call to prayer, that, united
in your Spirit, they may be used for the furtherance of
your kingdom and the glory of your holy name.

Muriel McDonald, Salisbury diocese, England

March 5th – Isadora, religious 5th century
Decade of Evangelism

O God our Father, thank you for bringing us together as a
family in your name. Go before us in all we do, unite us
in your love, that your blessing may be upon us in every
step we take. So dwell within us that we may go forth
with the light of hope in our eyes, your love in our hearts,
that strengthened by your grace we may seek to do your
will, through Jesus Christ, our Lord.

Delabole MU, Truro diocese, England

March 6th – Baldred/Billfrith/Cyniberg
For unity

We give thanks and praise to Almighty God for the work within this world through our Lord Jesus Christ, because even in our divided humanity, separated from each other, we experience now and then the reconciliation which comes from you; our thanks to you and praise can never end.

We ask you to accept us in your Son. Grant us the spirit of unity that takes away whatever comes to divide us. Keep us in union with all your people and make your Church become a sign of unity among all people. We pray all this through Jesus Christ, our Lord.

Janet Nyenda, East Ankole diocese, Uganda

March 7th – Perpetua and her companions, martyrs 203
Political prisoners

Merciful Father, be with all political prisoners; grant that they will not feel forgotten by the world at large; give them courage and hope in their ordeal; help them according to their needs, through Jesus Christ, our Lord.

Freda Howes, Winchester diocese, England

March 8th – Edward King, bishop and teacher 1910
For those in the hands of rebels

Almighty God, I pray for all those who are in the hands of the rebellious that you may free them and bring them home.
O God, may your love surround and your strength support them so that they may have faith and courage to endure.

May your blessing rest upon those who are in trouble, sorrow, sickness and need. Lord Jesus, send your blessing upon them and those who try to help them. Fill them with encouragement and peace through Jesus Christ, our Lord.

Besordu Bangura, Bo diocese, Sierra Leone

March 9th – Maqhamusela Khanyile of Zululand, martyr 1877
Scientific discoveries

Lord of all, I thank you for the wonder of the world that you have created. Open my eyes to the lessons that you can teach me as I go about my daily life, and help me to use those lessons to bring me into closer fellowship with you. I thank you for all the discoveries that science has made and pray that they may be used as a sacred trust to benefit mankind and bring glory to your name.

Maureen Sutton, Chester diocese, England

March 10th – Robert Machray, archbishop 1904
Noise versus the Lord's peace

The world is a noisy place, Lord – cars, buses and lorries roar past in the busy street; dustbins rattle and crash as they are emptied; women raise their voices above the ever-present intrusive background music and continuous bleep of cash registers in the bustling supermarket; trains, planes and lawnmowers stridently proclaim their presence; men hurl bombs, bullets and abuse at each other; everywhere, it's so noisy!

But you said, 'Be still and know that I am God' –

I know that you have created the quiet places, Lord. I have found the peace of the high mountain slopes, the tranquillity of a gentle river bank, the quiet of woodland and moor. Help me, Lord, to find that peace today; to take time off from my busy-ness to listen to your still small voice. Lord, grant me your peace.

Rochester diocese, England

March 11th – Auria, religious c.1100
Can I do something?

Can I even once a day do something – preferably
unnoticed and unthanked, something considerate,
something on my own initiative to make life easier for
someone else . . .?

It may be listening an extra half minute, or showing
concern, or offering advice, or even correction – usually
something small – but something every single day, for no
other reason than that I am christened. I bear Christ in
me. I play the part of Christ.

MU Young Families' department, United Kingdom

March 12th – Gregory the Great, bishop and teacher 604
For others

Lord, keep me cheerful despite adversity; make me ever
mindful of the needs of others during prosperity.

Chelmsford diocese, England

*March 13th – Keneopa and Manihera of Taranaki,
martyrs 1847*
Dull work

Lord, a lot of the work I have to do is dull, deadly dull.
Sometimes I'm so bored and sometimes I'm depressed. It
goes on day after day. God, sometimes I hate work. And
then I remember two things and take heart; I ask your
help to keep them more in mind.

I remember the carpenter's shop at Nazareth. That can't
always have been joy and sunshine. People can be very
rude to others who work for them, so I know that you
understand and I'm thankful. I remember, too, that my
work is linked to the work of others – to all people. They

depend on me and I depend on them. Lord, keep me
faithful.

MU Prayer Book, United Kingdom

March 14th – Mathilda, religious 968
Crisis in the economy

Almighty and everlasting Father, in whose hands are all
powers and kingdoms, we bless your name for the
goodness bestowed on man. Have mercy on all nations
that are presently experiencing crisis in their economies.
Revamp and stabilize their economies. Remove poverty
and scarcity from their lands and supply their needs
according to your riches in glory. Father, guide every
country in the proper management of her resources and
help them to use them judiciously, carefully and
objectively. Bless the natural and man-made resources of
every nation; in Jesus Christ's name we pray.

Mrs J. A. Ibimodi, Kwara diocese, Nigeria

*March 15th – Samuel and Henrietta Barnett, social
reformers 1913*
The unemployed

O Lord, our heavenly Father, we commend to your
protecting care and compassion the men and women of
this and every land now suffering distress and anxiety
through lack of work. Prosper, we pray, the counsel of
those engaged in the order of industrial life, that all
people may be set free from want and fear, and may be
enabled to work in security and peace, for the happiness
of the common life and the wellbeing of their countries.
Through Jesus Christ, our Lord.

Llandaff diocese, Wales

March 16th – Eusebia, abbess c.680
Money – planning ahead

Lord, the world of finance is so confusing. We're
concerned about our home, about crises of illness,
disability; and who will help when one of us dies? Will
we have enough money?

   We've had so much advice, some wrong advice; it's very
hard to know which course to take. Figures are thrown at
us too fast to take in and it's confusing.

   But most of all, Lord, there's never enough time to
understand it properly and people don't realize we're
slower now. Please help us not to be anxious about the
future, or too proud to ask for help. May we live each day
sure of your presence with us.

   Joined in Love, New Zealand

*March 17th – Patrick of Ireland, bishop and missionary
461*
For a young person away from home

O Lord, be with . . . . . wherever he/she is or whatever
he/she is doing. Watch over him/her and protect him/her.
Give him/her confidence, courage, patience, endurance,
compassion and understanding. If he/she meets with
temptation give him/her the will and the strength to resist
it; and help him/her to be tactful and respectful to his/her
superiors. Above all may he/she live his/her life to your
praise and glory. This we ask in the name of Jesus Christ,
our Lord.

   *Margaret Pollock, Down and Dromore diocese,
   Ireland*

March 18th – Cyril of Jerusalem, bishop and teacher 386
Being a Christian woman

My loving Lord, I thank you for being a Christian woman.
I pray especially for areas which it is really impossible to
share Christ with those of other faiths or of none. But
Lord, give me the strength to love them, to be kind to
them, so that day by day they may come close to you.

Four women from Kigezi diocese, Uganda

March 19th – ST JOSEPH OF NAZARETH
Prayer of a husband

Father! Yes, that's the right term with which to address
you. I too am a father. But I'm a husband first. I can't
really call you 'husband' but I'd like to because I want to
see you as a pattern for my husbanding. As you are Father
to us your children, so I am called to be father to my
children. And to who else should I look for a pattern for
my fathering but to you?

But husband! Maybe it's more difficult to be a husband
than a father. 'Christ laid down his life for his bride the
Church' – I remember the vicar saying that to us during
our wedding preparations. That's the pattern for every
husband.

Christ, help me to love my wife with the quality of
loving with which you loved your Church. Father, help me
to be father to my children as you are father to us all.

Chelmsford diocese, England

March 20th – Cuthbert, bishop and missionary 687
One makes a difference

I am only one, but still I am one. I cannot do everything
but still I can do something. And because I cannot do
everything let me not refuse to do something that I can

do. For one is the nucleus around which to gather a second, a third and a group.

So never say, 'What difference does one make?' – one person makes all the difference.

Salisbury diocese, England

March 21st – Thomas Cranmer, archbishop and martyr 1556
Use of our time

God, give us wisdom to use every day's opportunity. O God, give us a new heart that will daily trust in you, and remove all form of sin and pride from us.

O Lord, give us true humanity. Put the oil of the Holy Spirit in the lamp of our lives. Father, help us always to care for those in need or in danger and to pray for them.

Help all the Mothers' Union members so that we may be exemplary to others for your glory. We pray all this in the name of our Lord, Jesus Christ.

Revd Sesai Tibikaraho, Bunyoro-Kitara diocese, Uganda

March 22nd – Thomas Ken, bishop and poet 1711
My personal prayer

Forgive me, Lord, for not being good,
for forgetting to do the things that I should.

Forgive my short temper and grumpiness too,
and all the wrong things that I say and do.

Please help my faith to grow stronger each day,
to be much more worthy in every way.

To wear a smile instead of a frown,
to try and stay cheerful when things are down.

Help me to be joyful with your love in my heart,
and to show love to others as each day I start.

So thank you, Lord, for your loving care,
for being right with me everywhere.

I praise and bless your name alway,
throughout the minutes and hours of each day.

My faith will keep me striving on,
till the end of my life, forever Amen.
    Liz Curtis, Gloucester diocese, England

*March 23rd – Gregory the Illuminator, bishop and
missionary c.332*
The gift of sight

Lord Jesus, we thank you for the gift of sight. May we be
ever mindful how precious our eyes are and that we can
behold your beauty from season to season.

   Give to those who are blind, we pray, or who have
impaired vision an extra sense of feeling and touch, that
your care for them may be revealed in other ways.
    Catherine Eales, Bath and Wells diocese, England

March 24th – Oscar Romero, archbishop and martyr 1980
Friends in adversity

So fill us with your spirit, O Lord, to think and pray for
our friends who are in adversity, that they may grow from
strength to strength; finding the joy in you, Lord, to be
their strength; repelling promptly every thought of
discontent, anxiety, discouragement, self-seeking; and
cultivating cheerfulness in you and the habit of holy
silence and childlike faith in you, the Almighty. Through
Christ, our Saviour and advocate.
    Maranga Banda, Mzuzu, Lake Malawi diocese

March 25th – THE ANNUNCIATION
Lady Day

Lord, take me as I am with all my faults and failures, and make me what you want me to be. I give myself to you, my whole self: my gifts and my talents, my health and my intellect, and all my future days, that you may fulfil in me and through me your purpose for my life in the world and for your great glory.

   Freda Howes, Winchester diocese, England

March 26th – Harriet Monsell, religious 1811–1883
Mothering Sunday

Almighty God, Father of all creation, who chose Mary to be the Mother of our Lord, Jesus Christ, we give thanks for those who mother and nurture us. Following in her example of obedience and trust, give us grace to respond with love and affection to all those who seek our help and support. May we nurture the growth of a fuller Christian life in your world. Through Jesus Christ, our Lord.

   Winchester diocese, England

March 27th – Charles Henry Brent, bishop 1929
A prayer for the Mothers' Union

O Lord, our God, wherever you are allowed to be king there is peace and justice. We pray for your help in understanding our role as Mothers' Union members in your world. Strengthen our faith in your Lordship and purposes; deepen our commitment to set aside time to read your word and to pray; encourage us as we seek to uphold Christ's teaching on marriage and at the same time lovingly to support families in pain and disarray.

   Above all, Father, as we listen to your heartbeat and seek to keep in step with you, give us the strength and guidance of your Holy Spirit, through Jesus Christ, our Lord.

Val Brookes, Dublin and Glendalough diocese, Ireland

March 28th – Arthur Stanton, priest 1913
Lent

Teach us, O Lord, so to use this season of Lent that we may be drawn closer to you. Grant us grace to grow in holiness that our lives may be strengthened for your service and used for your glory. We ask this in your name.

Salisbury diocese, England

March 29th – John Keble, priest, pastor and poet 1866
For wisdom

Loving Father, we your children are here, failing to do your will. You have created us in your image and given us all the potential to do everything, but Lord we are failing. Give us wisdom so that we are able to understand and perform our duties as expected of us.

We have not done what you expect us to do because of ignorance. Give us wisdom, Father, to do your will. We pray all this in Jesus' name.

Revd Sesai Tibikaraho, Bunyoro-Kitara diocese, Uganda

March 30th – Osberga, abbess c.1016
Prayer for disobedient children

Heavenly God, I thank you for all types of gifts you give us. Send your Holy Spirit to the heart of all children who disobey their parents when giving them advice. When exchanging bad words with their parents, Lord, cool their hearts. Heavenly Father, give them love, so that your name may be praised.

Rohda Elikana, Maridi diocese, Sudan

March 31st – John Donne, priest and poet 1631
Use us, Lord

Lord Jesus, you are the light that lights up our darkness,
you comfort us when we are lonely. You take our failings
and turn them to strength, you lead us forward when we
lose our way, you take all our hurts and worries and you
carry us in times of need.

   Use us, Lord, to spread your message of love and
forgiveness.

   Sheila Abrahams, Lichfield diocese, England

APRIL

Sorrow and Joy

April 1st – Frederick Denison Maurice, priest and theologian 1872
Confession

O God, our Father, we have failed to be the people you
meant us to be.
We have not loved you with all our hearts;
we have not loved our neighbours as ourselves;
we are sorry for the opportunities to serve you that we
have missed;
we are sorry for the thoughts and words and deeds which
have been unkind and unloving;
we ask your forgiveness for all our sins,
through Jesus Christ, our Lord.
   MU Service Book, United Kingdom

April 2nd – Henry Budd, priest 1850

Dear God,
Forgive us what we have done wrong and remember about
the hungry people in the world and don't let anyone be
left out.
   Sara Benge (aged 7), Gloucester diocese, England

April 3rd – Richard of Chichester, bishop 1253
Release

A grey and chilly Sabbath morn,
no sunlight, no blue sky.
The birds were slow to greet the dawn,
but now they circled high.
The church seemed steeped in Lenten gloom,
the hymns were low-toned, sad,
in nave, near altar, not one bloom
to make a tired heart glad.

I turned my head, and in my pew
upon a father's arm
there was a child, so young, so new,
so full of infant charm.
And, by the Son of God's good grace
my spirit struggled free –
when, from out a baby's face
His eyes looked at me.
   Olwen Selby, Canterbury diocese, England

April 4th – Martin Luther King, prophet 1968
For prisoners

Merciful Father, be with those in our prisons who have
offended against the law. May they come to know your
love and forgiveness, and turn to you in true repentance,
that they may have hope for the future and the
opportunity of making a fresh start.

   Lord, be with all political prisoners; grant that they will
not feel forgotten by the world at large. Give them
courage and hope in their ordeal and help them according
to their needs.

   Through Jesus Christ, our Lord.
   Freda Howes, Winchester diocese, England

April 5th – Juliana of Mont Cornillon c.1258
Sliding into the pit

Lord, when I feel myself sliding into the pit . . . stay close;
sit with me in my silence and confusion, and give me your
shoulder to lean on. Prevent me from falling too far, and
in your good time, help me rise to my feet again.

   In Jesus' name. Amen.
   Birmingham diocese, England

April 6th – William Law, priest and mystic 1761
Those we find hard to like

Creator and Father of all, help us to love and care for those we find hard to like. Teach us to understand and befriend all who have been so hurt by life that they can only express themselves in hurtful ways.

Through Jesus Christ, our Lord, whose healing power brought wholeness of life to all who came to Him.

St Albans diocese, England

April 7th – William Muhlenberg, priest 1877 – Palm Sunday
Dare to give

O God our Father, you fill us with new life by the gift of your Holy Spirit; there is no end to the bounty of your love. In all our encounters with others, whether close or distant, long-lived or fleeting, help us dare to offer the best we can from your love in us; forgive our weakness when we fail to reveal as much of your joy as we could.

Through Him who dared all to reveal your boundless love, your Son, Jesus Christ, our Lord.

Edith Coulton, Newcastle diocese, England

April 8th – Saints and martyrs of the Americas
Prayer for a son serving in the armed forces

Dear Lord, please look after my boy. Don't let him come to any harm. Let him know that we love him, and we are thinking of him constantly. Please bring him home safely.

Sandie Giles, St Albans diocese, England

April 9th – Dietrich Bonhoeffer, pastor and theologian
1945

The Holy Spirit

Holy Spirit,
think through me
till your ideas
are my ideas.

   Oxford diocese, England

April 10th – Margery Kempe, visionary c.1373

For each other

Lord, help us to feel for each other;
help us to listen to each other;
help us to work for each other;
help us to love each other;
all for your sake.

   Rochester diocese, England

April 11th – George Augustus Selwyn, bishop and
missionary 1878

Maundy Thursday

Lord Jesus, show us how we may wash the feet, not of
your saints but of the humble and ordinary people among
whom we live and work, for whom we also pray and give
you thanks. Show us the right way to serve them because
they are yours, and in this service we are serving you.
Lord, we are not worthy to do you any service, but you
have given the commandment and we would obey.

   Daphne Fraser, MU Anthology of Public Prayers,
United Kingdom

April 12th – Clara Barton, social reformer 1912
Good Friday

It was your love, Lord Jesus, that caused you to be nailed to
the cross. It was your love that held you there when you might
have called for legions of angels. It was your love that pleaded
for your murderers and prayed, 'Father, forgive them'.

Help us, most gracious Lord, to grasp something more
of your love, to receive your forgiveness, and to learn to
forgive others even as we have been forgiven, for your
love's sake. Amen.
Birmingham diocese, England

April 13th – Margaret of Castello, mystic 1320
Thank you, Lord

Lord Jesus, thank you for showing us that
forgiveness is better than revenge,
love is stronger than hate,
self-sacrifice more desirable than self-preservation.
Lord, hold us in the victory of your forgiveness,
won so hardly for us on the cross,
that we being forgiven sinners
may forgive and love all those who seek to hurt us.
Gloucester diocese, England

April 14th – Lidwine, visionary 1380–1433
An Easter prayer

Reach out in spirit;
roll away the stone of doubt
and from the depths of faith,
receive the Risen Christ
in the sacrament
of this present moment.
Lorna Nevitt, Portsmouth diocese, England

April 15th – Padarn, bishop 6th century
Alleluia

In every morning sunrise, we thank you, O Lord.
In every bird that sings, we thank you, O Lord.
In every friend who takes time to listen, we thank you,
O Lord.
In every evening sunset, we thank you, O Lord.
For music, dance and drama, we thank you, O Lord.
For good health and vision, we thank you, O Lord.
Alleluia, Alleluia.
  Mrs M. E. Baggs, London diocese, England

April 16th – Bernadette of Lourdes, visionary 1879
During the service of Holy Communion

O God our Father, I thank you for giving me health and
strength to come to this Holy Communion service. I pray
for the strengthening and refreshing of my soul by the
Body and Blood of Christ, as my body would be by bread
and wine.

  Help me to follow the example of your dear Son, by
trying to help others at all times. Show me the
opportunities as they present themselves and give me the
courage to act upon them, through Jesus Christ, our
Lord.
  Margaret Pollock, Down and Dromore diocese,
  Ireland

April 17th – Donnan, monk and martyr 617
About to be married

Lord, guide those about to be married. Help them to face
their future together with love, patience and
understanding. Lead them through life with your love,

and bring them richness and fulfilment in their precious
gift of marriage.

*Margaret Bloomfield, St Edmundsbury and Ipswich
diocese, England*

April 18th – Kateri Tekakwitha, mystic 1680
For the bride and groom on their wedding day

Our loving Father, it is wonderful to share this day, for
which we have waited so eagerly. We thank you for your
sweet and mysterious gift of love; for all that we find in
each other, that strengthens and enriches. Make our
relationship, begun in your presence and gladdened by
family and friends gathered this day within the church,
strong, holy and everlasting. Bless the life that we plan,
and build and keep together; let it ever be open to things
true and beautiful and joyous. Let us so love and trust you
in the light, that if dark skies are ever above us, we shall
remember how near you are, how loving and how
dependable.

In the name of Jesus, our Lord and Saviour, we fashion
this simple prayer.

Martin and Carol Riddett, Llandaff diocese, Wales

April 19th – Alphege, archbishop and martyr 1012
Strengthening of marriage

Lord, in the day-to-day living of marriage may husbands
and wives never take each other for granted. May their
love remain strong to withstand the pressures of today's
world. In times of stress or tension may they constantly
find renewal in the strength of your love, and in times of
joy to praise and bless your holy name. For the sake of
Jesus Christ, our Lord.

Portsmouth diocese, England

April 20th – Beuno, abbot c.640
The in-laws

O God our Father, we ask you to bless those who have entered our family life through marriage. We pray that our different backgrounds may bring enrichment and a deeper understanding. Take away mistrust, suspicion and possessiveness, and guide us by your Spirit into a new bond of love and affection, through Christ, our Lord.

MU Prayer Book, United Kingdom

April 21st – Anselm, archbishop 1109
Second marriage

In the stillness of this moment I hold my breath, and marvel at the wonder of this second chance in marriage.

God, thank you for this second time of marriage. We each accept all that has gone before. We pledge ourselves to this new love. May our experiences and differences take on a positive value, that through them we may enrich our lives as we learn from one another.

Thank you for our past, for the pains and for the joys.

Thank you for your blessing on us now. May we continue to know this blessing and may it always be part of our lives together.

Joined in Love, New Zealand

April 22nd – Pherburtha, martyr c.341
For polygamous homes

Forgive us, loving Father, for our sins, but especially for gluttony: men are not satisfied by one woman; women hope to get wealth from men. Men acquire land in different places to get wealth, thus having many women. Father, satisfy them with your heavenly grace so that the income they get is enough. Teach them to love faithfully and stick to one woman. Look upon the existing polygamous homes and speak to them to show the glory of God by making proper homes; teach other people not to take that way. Let the unmarried get proper and happy marriages, for your glory.

Revd Sesai Tibikaraho, Bunyoro-Kitara diocese, Uganda

April 23rd – George of England, martyr c.304
For courage

Heavenly Father, give us a cheerful heart and courage to stand for all that is fair, good and true in our society. Help us always to speak out where we see injustice, for Jesus' sake.

Revd Hazel Hughes, Worcester diocese, England

April 24th – Toyohiko Kagawa, teacher and evangelist 1960
Prayer about war

Almighty and everlasting God, heavenly Father, we thank you for your great love to us. I pray you to change the hearts of those who like their problems to be solved in the way of war. By killing innocent people all over the world and making themselves glad when destroying most of the important places, they have forgotten you.

Living God, forgive them all and send your Holy Spirit to open their hearts and minds so that if they carry their troubles to you all can be solved a peaceful way.

I pray you to save your innocent people during all this sad time and protect them, through Christ, our Lord.

Yodita Elisa, Maridi diocese, Sudan

April 25th – ST MARK THE EVANGELIST
Loss of a close friend

O everlasting Lord, we pray in great sorrow and pain after the loss of our close friend. We know that, Lord God, you are ever with us in times of joy, sorrow and happiness. We ask that you may let us stand upright to whatever comes. In your name everything is possible.

For our dear friend whom you have called, we pray that his/her family may have their pain eased and know that all good things come to an end. Let your loving wisdom and almighty power work in them the good purpose of your perfect will. We pray that we may come back to our usual peace, liberty and unity, plus community co-operation. We ask this in your name.

Four women from Kabale, Kigezi diocese, Uganda

April 26th – Stephen of Perm, bishop 1345–1396
For all who suffer

Father, we pray for all who are suffering: the many suffering the violence of war, the hungry, the homeless and all who have lost their loved ones and all means of earning, the oppressed and fearful.

Lord God, the protector of all who trust in you, fill our hearts and the hearts of all people with your love and compassion.

We bring before you the sufferings of your children throughout the world; may they be aware of your presence and may we be united with them in their needs and in their suffering.

Edinburgh diocese, Scotland

April 27th – Zita of Lucca, defender of the destitute
c.1278
Love our enemies

Dear Lord, you have taught us to love our enemies and to
do good to those who hate us. We pray for all terrorists.
We remember that you died for them too. Take from their
hearts all evil thoughts and help them to see that the
power of love is stronger than the bomb and the bullet.
Lead them from violence into your ways of peace.
    Lord, in your mercy, hear our prayer.
    Rochester diocese, England

April 28th – Osanna of Cattano, visionary 1565
Fear of violence, war, starvation and sudden death

Merciful Father, we place into your hands all those with
needy hearts and souls, those whose hope is gone and
whose life is spent. We want to remember those who are
suffering both in body and spirit; those in war-affected
areas, craving for peace and understanding between men.
We pray that you put into all men a real desire for peace,
and the earth filled with the knowledge of your love.
    We also place into your hands those people who have
no food. We ask that you may give us a giving hand that
we may love to share with those who don't have help.
    We also want to remember those who have lost their
beloved ones. Be their source of comfort, Lord, and fill
the gaps of the gone.
    Lord, with the guidance of the Holy Spirit, we pray that
we may be helped to look to you for all our needs. In your
name we have prayed.
    Four women from Kigezi diocese, Uganda

April 29th – Catherine of Sienna, teacher and mystic 1380
Make us yours

O living God, giver of light and joy, enter into our lives
and make us yours. Be our light that we may see clearly
all that is good and all that is wise.
May our lives be bright with your glory.
May our words be kind with your tenderness.
May our deeds be good with your holiness.
May our minds be wise with your wisdom.
May our hearts be filled with your peace.
  Gloucester diocese, England

April 30th – Heni Te Kirikaramu 1864
Channels of joy and hope

Lord, use us to be channels of joy and hope to all your
people: to the lonely and the sad, to the sick, the anxious
and the bereaved. Use us to become channels of your love
in whatever way is needful; and ever to radiate the peace
and joy of your presence.
  Lucy Davies, Llandaff diocese, Wales

MAY

Young Shoots

May 1st – SS. PHILIP AND JAMES, APOSTLES

Dear God, I love you.

Sally Remmer (aged 4), Gloucester diocese, England

May 2nd – Athanatius, bishop and teacher 1003
Pram service

Father in heaven, whose Son Jesus Christ showed His love for children by taking them in His arms and blessing them, take these your children, we pray you, and those who care for them, in your loving arms so that they may continue to be yours for ever, and daily increase in your Holy Spirit. Through our Lord, Jesus Christ, with the Father and the Holy Spirit; One God, present with us for ever.

The Mothers' Union, Province of Ireland

May 3rd – Elisabeth Leseur, spiritual writer 1914
For children

Lord Jesus, you desire a life of harmony and devotion in little children to be developed as they grow, since your kingdom belongs to them. I therefore commit them into your hands, so that in the end they will glorify your name. I also pray that you will bless them so that they will know you and give their lives to you as they hear your word.

Joanna Cofie, The Gambia diocese

May 4th – Monica, mother of Augustine of Hippo 387
Caring for children

Help us, Lord, to have patience with our children.
Help us, Lord, to recognize their difficulties and to help and guide them.
Help us to be tolerant of their untidiness.

Help us to teach them compassion and love towards their fellow beings.
Help them through the temptations that are presented to them in today's society.

Salisbury diocese, England

May 5th – Asaph, bishop 6th century
Be with me

Dear Lord, as I open my eyes on another day, please accompany me on my way. Please grant me understanding and encourage me to do your will, so that when evening falls again you may grant me rest and quietness. Thank you, Lord.

St Asaph diocese, Wales

May 6th – Benedicta of Rome 6th century
For our children's education

Our loving Father, I pray for the children in our country who are still young but unable to continue with their studies because of the problem of no money for school dues. Comfort them, show them your precious love; help them to put their hope into you, and save their lives; find a way for them to survive in the world.

I also pray for the students who finish their studies and then delay or fail to get jobs. Give them patience and remind them to keep on praying without getting tired.

Fulfil your promise because in the scriptures it says that to those who pray will be given. I bring this prayer before you with all my faith, through your Son, Jesus Christ.

Revd Sesai Tibikaraho, Bunyoro-Kitara diocese, Uganda

May 7th – Stanislaus of Cracow, bishop and martyr 1079
Prayer for children without parents

God our Father, all parenthood comes from you. Allow
all the children who have lost their parents to understand
your love for the world; send your Holy Spirit to lead
them in their ways. Through Christ, our Lord.
 Lucy Timatio, Maridi diocese, Sudan

May 8th – Julian of Norwich, mystic c.1417
For women in the church

Jesus, word of the Father, born of a woman, who in your
days here on earth companied with Martha and Mary in
their home at Bethany, we ask your blessing on the homes
from which we have come and to which we shall return.
As we meet together in fellowship we pray that we may
know your presence with us and find strength and
refreshment to serve you better in our daily lives. This we
ask for your love's sake.
 Nan Deedes, Winchester diocese, England

May 9th – Gregory of Nazianzus, bishop and teacher 389
Prayer for Church work

Our heavenly Father, we thank you for the ministry you
started in the death and resurrection of your Son, Jesus
Christ, our Lord. We thank you for the mission He left
with your Church before He ascended to you.

We therefore pray for the Church work in the world and
more especially for the voluntary workers among our
communities and villages. Guide them, Lord, to be your
true witnesses in their lives and deeds. We pray for those
with whom they work that they will have thirsty souls to
receive your word.

We pray trusting that you will hear our prayers,

through the name of our Lord and Saviour, Jesus Christ.
Marion Sebuhinja, Muhabura diocese, Uganda

May 10th – Rogation
A prayer for the seasons

Father, thank you for the spring; for the flowers, trees and other plants, and for the new-born animals.
Thank you for summer; for long, hot and lazy days in the sun.
Thank you for autumn; for the beautiful colours, for the forests and plains.
Thank you for winter; for times spent playing with friends in the snow, for Christmas-time spent with relatives.
Thank you for everything large and small that you created.
Valerie (aged 13), Chelmsford diocese, England

May 11th – Ruatara, Te ara mo te Rongopai ('The gateway for the Gospel')
For schoolchildren

Thank you, Lord, for the joy of children in the home. Thank you for their everyday growth, physically and spiritually. Have mercy and touch their hearts and minds as they go to school at the primary, secondary and post-secondary levels. Lord, help them not to go astray; lead them to choose the right companions; help them to be obedient and God-fearing. Give them your blessings in all their efforts; help, Lord, to change the lives of those that fall below expectation for good. Through Jesus Christ, our Lord, we pray.
Mrs R. A. Gbadeyan, Kwara diocese, Nigeria

May 12th – Florence Nightingale, nurse and social reformer 1910

Making a difficult choice

Holy Spirit, help and guide me. I don't know which choice to make: both are possible, and both are good. I want to know which is God's will. Help me to clear my mind so that I will see without prejudice; increase my love so that my choice will be guided by love of you. I am confused and need guidance. When, with your aid, I have chosen, stop me from looking back with regret and give me courage to go on fearlessly, trusting that I have done what is right and what is your will.

Welford-on-Avon MU, Gloucester diocese, England

May 13th – Ihaia Te Ahu, priest and missionary c.1823–1895

Working wives and mothers

Our loving Master and God, we thank you for making us women, and for the joy of being a wife and/or mother. In these times, Lord, many women have to hold jobs or run businesses in addition to the arduous responsibilities of running their homes. We need your special grace and blessing to be able to be successful both at home and at work; we often neglect one for the other. Lord, help us to so organize and manage our time and homes that we will be able to progress at our various jobs. Give us the spirit and heart that is easily content with what has been given to us by you, so that we are not blinded by envy and selfish drive. We pray in Jesus' name.

Dr S. O. Malomo, Kwara diocese, Nigeria

May 14th – ST MATTHIAS THE APOSTLE
'At home' mum

Lord give me:
Strength to cope when I feel like turning my back,
Wisdom to sort out quarrels,
Calm when the children fight and argue,
Love when I feel like hating,
Reassurance that I will get everything done,
Peace when life is full of interruptions,
The ability to be friends with my children,
Hope when every day seems the same,
Control when I feel like shouting,
Humility when I am in the wrong,
Joy that I am loved.
   Chelmsford diocese, England

May 15th – Dympna, martyr 7th century
For foster children and foster parents

Bless and guard all fostered children of all races and
creeds and give them reassurance in every situation. As
they grow up give them an understanding of the love and
concern there has been for them from both their social
workers and foster parents.

   To those who care for them give wisdom, compassion
and an endless capacity for joyful loving.

   Dear God, above all give us all real concern for these
your children in the community, and help us to take a
share of caring for them in whatever way we can.
   Salisbury diocese, England

May 16th – Te Wera Hauraki, missionary 19th century
Our adopted child

God, source of life and love, we thank you for this new child, not born to us but given to us to love and to call our own.

Be with . . . . .'s birth mother. May she know peace and strength in her decision. May she have the assurance that we will love and care for this child, so precious in your sight.

As . . . . . grows and asks questions may we always be honest and open. May our home be a place of friendship and outreach, acceptance and love.

Joined in Love, New Zealand

May 17th – Wiremu Te Tauri, missionary 19th century
Time for God when stressed

I'm hurt and miserable today, Lord. I can't see the joy in your world. Everything's gone wrong. Why is it that others can't see my point of view? I'm tense and worried; so busy, rushing; my brain working so hard. Help me to be calm, to give myself time to think. Why am I like this, Lord? . . .

Now that I have made time to listen I have heard your answer to my question, Lord. My thoughts were all of myself, all about me. Just for a moment they were about you. I can see a glimmer of light in the darkness. You have so much time for me; let me have more time for you.

MU Prayer Book, United Kingdom

May 18th – Tamihana Te Rauparaha, missionary 1876
One-parent families

Lord God, we offer to you the children living with only one parent. Help them to feel your love, and be with them in their times of confusion and loneliness.

Give strength, patience and wisdom to the parents trying to be both father and mother to their children, at the same time as they face up to their own needs.

Help us in the family of the Church to be open and caring with these families, as with all the families we know, through Jesus Christ, our Lord.

Christine McMullen, MU Anthology of Public Prayers, United Kingdom

May 19th – Dunstan, archbishop 988
Children, grandchildren and godchildren

Lord Jesus, we bring to you our children, grandchildren and godchildren that you may touch and bless them. Help us to be sensitive to their needs that they may grow up in the security of love, firm in faith and strong and straight in life.

Grant that we, and all who have a hand in training and teaching young people, may help and encourage them to become the people you intend them to be, to your honour and glory.

Sarah James, MU Anthology of Public Prayers, United Kingdom

May 20th – Alcuin, abbot and deacon 804
Ascension

Let us fix our eyes on Jesus, the author and protector of our faith, who for the joy set before Him endured the cross, scorning its shame, and sat down at the right hand of God.

Consider Him who endured such opposition from sinful men, so that you will not grow weary and lose heart.

Marjorie Hodbod, Blackburn diocese, England

May 21st – Helena and Constantine, protectors of the Faith 330 and 337
Growing up

Dear Father, as our children grow more independent, please help us to hold them with open arms; to provide a stable base to which they can return at any time. Keep us from questions or interfering, so that as we share love and trust with them, they may be open to the promptings of your love.

Rochester diocese, England

May 22nd – Rota Waitoa, priest 1853
Temptation

Living Lord, when you were in the desert you were tempted and yet won the victory. Give your strength to your people who can so easily be led astray. Lead them, instead, to those who will encourage them to follow your way of life. May they feel both wanted and loved, and be given opportunities to use their talents. When the world seems against them, give them the assurance that there is a God who cares for them.

London diocese, England

May 23rd – Frederick Augustus Bennett, bishop 1950
For ourselves

Heavenly Father, help us to be vigilant in our own lives, so that by neither word nor action may we be guilty of causing others to fall.

London diocese, England

May 24th – John and Charles Wesley, priests and teachers 1791 and 1788
For young people going out into the world

Lord Jesus, we pray for young people as they go out into the world. Help them be strong and courageous against the pressures and temptations of daily life. Give them a clear vision, a sense of rightness and grace to persevere. For Jesus Christ's sake.
   Portsmouth diocese, England

May 25th – Venerable Bede, monk and teacher 735
Understanding each other

O God, who has granted youth to see visions and age to dream dreams, help both young and old to understand each other. May those who are young be courteous to the aged; may those who are older look with sympathy upon new ideas, so that both young and old may work together for the coming of your kingdom.
   MU Prayer Book, United Kingdom

May 26th – Augustine of Canterbury, archbishop and missionary 605
Split families

Heavenly Father, we want to thank you for our homes and families; for it was your plan that all should live together in families for mutual love and help, and for encouragement in good living. We pray that you may give understanding to split families, and may you guide them and open their eyes so that they may turn to you as the builder of broken homes. Melt the hearts of the hard-hearted ones who do not want to come to a compromise that they may come to know you as their Lord and Saviour. Through Jesus Christ, our Lord.
   Four women from Kigezi diocese, Uganda

May 27th – John Calvin, theologian and reformer 1564
Unhappy homes

Loving Father, we pray for homes which are no longer
happy; where marriage and family life have broken down,
where children are torn in their love and loyalties to
parents, which causes them great distress. We pray for the
counselling services who try to ease these tensions; guide
teachers and give them patience and understanding
towards children who come from unhappy homes.

Portsmouth diocese, England

May 28th – Lanfranc, archbishop and abbot 1089
Worshipping alone

Dear Lord and Father, I ask your love and guidance for
all single members of the family who come to church on
their own. I feel very warmed and comforted by the other
members of the congregation and know I do not pray
alone. But, dear God, please help the other members of
my family who do not seek your love. Help them to open
their hearts and minds to you; I want to share my faith
and joy but they do not listen. I ask this in the name of
your Son, Jesus Christ, who died to save us all.

Joy Edwards, Monmouth diocese, Wales

May 29th – Bona of Pisa, religious 1207
For patience

Dear Lord, in this busy world we are all rushing
about full of our own importance, thinking that we are
the busiest people about and that what we think is best.

Help me to stop and listen to those about me: to have
patience to listen to the elderly who have lots to tell us,
and to children who have exciting things to relate. Give

us patience when we are tired and frustrated – when we are short of time.

You are patient with us. Please help me to be likewise, patient with those about me. For your name's sake.

Mainly Prayers, MU Young Families' department, United Kingdom

May 30th – Joan of Arc, martyr 1431
Pentecost

The Spirit of God is like the wind.
The wind makes yachts move
  Spirit of God, get me moving.
The wind blows rubbish around
  Spirit of God, blow away the rubbish from my life.
The wind dries the washing
  Spirit of God, make me useful.
The wind makes balloons fly high in the sky
  Spirit of God, lift me up to a new freedom.
The wind holds birds in the air
  Spirit of God, hold me in your love.
The wind turns windmills to grind the corn
  Spirit of God, give me strength to work for you.
The wind blows umbrellas inside out
  Spirit of God, be with me when I struggle.
The Spirit of God is like the wind:
  lively and cleansing, useful and strong.

Christine McMullen, MU Anthology of Public Prayers, United Kingdom

May 31st – Visit of the Blessed Virgin Mary to Elisabeth
Prayer for those who are pregnant

Heavenly Father, giver of all good things, give to those who are pregnant your abundant grace, strength and courage to carry the pregnancy with joy, peace and good health to full term. Be there at the time of labour to guide and guard them, and to grant them safe delivery. We ask all this in Jesus' name.

   Mrs A. M. Osaji, Kwara diocese, Nigeria

JUNE

The Earth

June 1st – Justin, martyr c.165
Each new day

Heavenly Father, we thank you for each new day in which we can
praise you – for the beauty of the earth;
learn more – about your teachings;
listen more – to your speaking;
and love you more through loving others.
  Brenda Thorpe, York diocese, England

June 2nd – The martyrs of Lyons 177
For the restoration of the world

Heavenly Father, creator of all things, who rejoiced in your creation at the beginning of the world; forgive us our sins of greed, selfishness and carelessness by which we daily damage the beauty to which we have become insensitive.

By war and violence we destroy families and their means of livelihood. We cut down great forests that are the homes of people, animals and birds. We ill-treat our farm animals in the race to outstrip our rivals in food production, yet still leave millions of people starving. We pollute our air and water with the excess of our greed, without thought for the disposal of what we waste.

For all this we ask not only forgiveness, but also the power to turn away from our headlong course of destruction, and instead to share in your constant work of creation, in preparation for the time when your kingdom comes on earth as it is in heaven.

This we ask through Jesus Christ, our Saviour, who Himself became part of your creation and gave His life for the whole world.
  Helen Lamb, Meath and Kildare diocese, Ireland

June 3rd – Martyrs of Uganda 1886 and 1978
Hard times

Please Father, teach me to understand the hard times in
my life; also prepare me for a life of service to you. Help
me to be realistic, but not unreasonably fearful, in
tackling any assignment you give to me.

   Janet Nyenda, East Ankole diocese, Uganda

June 4th – John XXIII, bishop and reformer 1963
The environment

O Lord, give mankind the desire and knowledge to take
more balanced care of the environment, which is
God-sent:
to deep-clean the waters and seas;
to preserve the rainforests for the birds and bees and
creatures yet unseen;
to love and consider the needs of all and not only man's
selfish needs.

   Carlisle diocese, England

June 5th – Boniface, bishop and martyr 754
War and starvation

Our heavenly Father, we beseech you for help to keep
away war and starvation from our country, for we know
that during war there is famine, sickness and acute
disharmony within the people. Deliver us from the evil
intentions of those who preach division in our country;
save us from starvation and sickness; and let us live in
harmony, peace and tranquillity so that your will shall
prevail in our nation. In Jesus' name we pray.

   Mrs V. B. Okunrintemi, Kwara diocese, Nigeria

June 6th – William Broughton, bishop 1853
Unity

O God, three in one, in you we see perfect unity and love.
We thank you for the unity that binds all Christians
together, regardless of their race, colour, language or
background.

We thank you that the Mothers' Union witnesses to this
worldwide unity in diversity. May we, and all your
people, be living signs of the peace and wholeness you
long for your world to know; and accept our worship and
our praise, this day, and always.

Coventry diocese, England

June 7th – Colman of Dromore, abbot and bishop
6th century
Trinity

Holy, blessed and glorious Trinity, our God,
your world gleams and resounds with your beauty.
Father, guide us to live in love with all creation;
Son, teach us to accept the cost of that love;
Spirit, show us yourself in everything and every person.

Jean Walker, St Albans diocese, England

June 8th – Agnes of Prague, religious 1281
God is great

Father, we praise you, you are full of glory, majesty, power
and joy; goodness and love eternal. You perform miracles
and give judgements, you protect us and do mighty acts.

Help us, Lord, to worship you and rejoice, and never to
forget the new Covenant which you made through your
wonderful Son, Jesus. Help us to be glad in you, to sing
your praise, to tell others about you, to bow down in
reverence, and to spend time quietly with you each day.

We ask this in the name of Jesus, your Son.
Marjorie Hodbod, Blackburn diocese, England

June 9th – Columba of Iona, abbot and missionary 597
Hands for work

Lord Jesus, I give you my hands to do your work.
I give you my feet to go your way.
I give you my eyes to see as you do.
I give you my tongue to speak your words.
I give you my mind that you may think in me.
I give you my spirit that you may pray in me.
Above all, I give you my heart that you may love in me
your Father and all mankind.
I give you my whole self that you may grow in me so that
it is you, Lord Jesus, who live and work and pray in me.
Guildford diocese, England

June 10th – Ephrem of Edessa, deacon 373
For travellers

God of Abraham, God of Isaac and of Jacob, who blessed
Jacob on his way to Laban his uncle, bless those who will
travel on land, water and in the air. Lead all of them
safely to their destinations and let them be blessed.

We remember those who cannot leave their home
because of ill-health or old age; be close to them, Lord, to
let them know they are not forgotten by you. We pray in
the name of Jesus Christ, our Lord.
Rhoda Ade Olarewaju, Kwara diocese, Nigeria

June 11th – ST BARNABAS THE APOSTLE
Choosing leaders

O God, our Father, who through your Son chose twelve disciples here on earth to spread your work and to inspire others to follow you; we ask you to guide us in our choice of office-bearers in this group/branch/parish/diocese.

   Give wisdom to those who vote, and courage and vision to those who take office, so that they may carry out your work in . . . . ..

   We ask this in the name of your Son, Jesus Christ, our Lord.

   The Mothers' Union, Province of Ireland

June 12th – Jolenta of Gnesen, religious 1298
Fill us

Lord of the tempest – fill us with your calm.
Lord of the fountain – fill us with living water.
Lord of the manger – fill us with new life.
Lord of the cross – fill us with sacrificial love.
Lord of the empty tomb – fill us with resurrection power.

   Rochester diocese, England

June 13th – Antony of Padua, teacher and missionary 1231
Loneliness

When I am sad and lonely, Lord, come to me.
When the darkness of the night seems so long, Lord, come to me.
When I wake up at dawn, feeling calm and so refreshed, then I know in my heart – Lord, you have comforted me.

   Marian Robson, Llandaff diocese, Wales

June 14th – Basil the Great, bishop and teacher 379
Prayer for travellers

Almighty and everlasting Father, we thank you for calling us to know your mercy and to have faith in you. I ask you to guide all those who travel by air, by sea, by road, by rail and by foot. Help them to remember you in their difficulties, and when they are tired, let them know that when our Lord was on this earth He faced every difficulty because you were with Him.

Allow us to follow Him and rise with Him at the end, through Christ, our Lord.

Rohda Elikana, Maridi diocese, Sudan

June 15th – Evelyn Underhill, mystic 1941
I will be there

I looked for Him in the soft petalled rose, I lifted my eyes to the sky,
I travelled far in my loneliness, please God don't pass me by.
I searched deep in a limpid pool, I watched the soft falling rain,
I gazed into the eyes of a new-born child, but my search was all in vain.
My soul cried out, 'Where next to look to find your guiding hand?
Give me strength to travel on to find the promised land.'
A small voice deep inside of me said, 'Have faith, do not despair,
believe in me, give me your heart and I will always be there.'

Eileen Fairclough, Wakefield diocese, England

June 16th – Joseph Butler, bishop 1752
Lord of all

Lord of the Spirit, come into my heart, like a breath of
wind.
Lord of all might, let my heart be strong, like the strength
of granite.
Lord of forgiveness, cleanse me of my sins, as the tide
flows over the sands.
Lord of peace, still my heart, as the calm of still waters.
   Norma Astley, Truro diocese, England

June 17th – Tarasia of Lorvao, religious 1211
Flower arranger's prayer

O Lord, who has created all,
each leaf and blossom, great and small,
look down and bless my work this day,
guide my eyes and hands, I pray,
that I within your house may make
an offering worthy of your sake.
   Oxford diocese, England

June 18th – Bernard Mizeki, martyr and missionary 1896
Skill with hands

Christ Jesus, at your carpenter's bench you knew the joy
fulfilled by creating with your hands. I thank you for my
hands and the skills you have given me, and the
opportunities to care for others in your name.
   Chelmsford diocese, England

June 19th – Sadhu Sundan Singh, evangelist and teacher 1929
Museums and art galleries

Most merciful Father, who so created man that in art he might voice that which is beyond speech; we praise you for museums and art galleries. Bless all who are connected with them in any way. We pray that by such works of art, we may be brought to share together in a richer life, so that we may praise you in a fuller dedication to your service, through Jesus Christ, our Lord.

Rochester diocese, England

June 20th – Edward of West Saxons, martyr 978
Church cleaners' prayer

Heavenly Father, whose only Son, Jesus Christ, shared in the everyday tasks of life, accept and bless our work in this place of worship. Help us, like your servant Dorcas, to find fulfilment in your service, through Jesus Christ, our Lord.

The Mothers' Union, Province of Ireland

June 21st – Henare Wiremu Taratoa 1864
Praise

Father, we thank you and honour your name. Help us, Lord, to see how much you have done for us and learn to worship and praise your name. Help us, Lord, to know that you will never leave us to handle our problems alone, because you care for us.

East Ankole diocese, Uganda

June 22nd – Alban, martyr c.304
The communion of saints

Father, joining hands with all your family, I worship you –
with angels and archangels who serve continually in your
presence; with that whole communion of your saints, who
now see you face-to-face; with all your people still on
pilgrimage, from the farthest corners of the earth. Within
this great fellowship of your children, I am never alone.

Jean Walker, St Albans diocese, England

June 23rd – Wiremu Tamihana, prophet 1866
Decade of Evangelism

Here we are in another decade,
will it be different from the last?
Can we learn from mistakes past,
will we reap from the price we have paid?
  Help us Lord.

There is always war somewhere year after year,
precious lives lost of someone held dear.
Loved ones held hostage – where is the gain?
Others lie helpless or writhing in pain.
  Help them, Lord.

So many hungry – and homeless too,
so much poverty it doesn't seem true.
If this is progress in this day and age –
all I can say is, it fills me with rage.
  What can I do, Lord?

I care, I care, but what can I do?
The little I give will help so few.
So I will continue to pray day by day –
for understanding, patience, hope, trust, and say –
  Our Father, your will be done.
  Peggy Bennett, Worcester diocese, England

June 24th – BIRTH OF JOHN THE BAPTIST
Sharing Christ with our neighbours

Almighty and everlasting God, I pray that you guide me and help me overcome the problem of sharing Christ with my neighbours, most of whom are non-believers. Give me courage to proclaim your name that they may know you and get your salvation. Give me courage to proclaim your love and care to families who have lost many relatives and are in despair, so that they may trust in you more and more. Guide me and help me to share Christ to AIDS patients who have lost hope in life so that I may make your name known to them and lead them to your cross and salvation.

Four women from Kigezi diocese, Uganda

June 25th – Dorothty of Montau, pilgrim 1399
For women's groups

O God, let our women's groups have the love to support each other in all their work in your Church, as well as in various voluntary works in different communities, villages, towns and cities. Help them to share Christ with their neighbours as Christian women in all that they do. In Jesus' name we pray.

Rhoda Ade Olarewaju, Kwara diocese, Nigeria

June 26th – Ember Days
A Conference prayer

Lord Jesus Christ, we praise you for your goodness to us. Guide our preparation for our Conference; be with those who are to speak to us, that what they say may stimulate our vision of our work.

Be with those who will attend the Conference, that it may be a time for refreshment, fellowship and a reawakening of ourselves to see your will for us in the future.

Ripon diocese, England

June 27th – Cyril of Alexandria, theologian 444
For the rulers of our countries

Almighty God, who created this world and entrusted it to the children of men, we ask you to give its rulers the wisdom from above and goodwill to lead it with justice, righteousness and truth. Deliver us, we pray, from faithlessness and fear; save us from fighting and wars which are more and more driving our nations to darkness and despair and misery.

Raise up Christian rulers, we pray O Lord, and strengthen those rulers who strive after unity and brotherhood, and risk their lives to establish righteousness and peace in the time when most people are striving after their own glory, using the weapon of division.

Dear Lord, break down all barriers which divide the rulers from the ruled, that they may walk and work together in one accord with each other and with you. We pray trusting in you, Lord.

Byumba diocese, Rwanda

June 28th – Irenaeus, bishop and martyr c.200
True witnesses

O Lord, who knows all our hopes as well as all our failures, uphold us in all we do with the power of your love, that we may be true witnesses to you. To your honour and glory.

Gisele Ridgeway, York diocese, England

June 29th – ST PETER THE APOSTLE
The Rock

The rock stands gaunt and black,
towering above the waves, like a sentry on guard against
all enemies;
solid and strong and immovable in the face of all the fury
that the foaming sea hurls upon it.
That rock has stood for many thousands of years,
witnessed many things.
Ships have been wrecked in storms;
countless men and women have endeavoured to scale its
face;
birds have nested in its crevices;
and yet it still stands firm.
Lord, you once called one of your disciples 'The Rock' –
a man who denied you three times when faced with
danger –
and yet you called Peter 'The Rock'.
I am weak and easily frightened – I find it
difficult to keep my faith when I face danger.
Help me to be your Rock, to stand firm for you,
against all that the world may hurl at me.
Lord, the one true Rock, help me.

Rochester diocese, England

June 30th – *Martyrdom of Paul*
Praise when life is painful

Lord Jesus, help me to find something to praise you for
even when life is very painful. May other people learn
from me something of your love, your strength and your
wisdom.

Peterborough diocese, England

JULY

The Middle Years

July 1st – Mary Teresa Dease, religious 1889
Always there

Heavenly Father, I thank you for the knowledge that you are always there for me; that no matter what I do, I can still turn back to you with repentance in my heart. But most of all, I thank you for your everlasting love and protection over me. In Jesus' name I pray.

George diocese, South Africa

July 2nd – Maria Storioni, religious 1399
One day at a time

To meet life one day at a time, one step at a time;
to have the strength and the will to keep on keeping on;
to have the wisdom to handle the affairs of life;
to have the ability to make right and good decisions;
to have the courage to let the past go, to forge ahead resolutely;
to have the grace to meet each experience; expectantly, happily;
to have the faith to know there is no loss or separation in God, that in Him I am forever with those I love;
to have the vision to see the good in all things, the Christ in all persons;
to have an awareness of God's presence, close, abiding;
to know that underneath are the everlasting arms, that God will not fail me nor forsake me;
this is my prayer.

Salisbury diocese, England

July 3rd – ST THOMAS THE APOSTLE
Passing on our faith

Father God, we thank you that you are the same yesterday, today and forever; hallowed be your name. You have shown mercy to each generation; be merciful to us in our time we pray. Forgive us for the way your name is dishonoured, and help us to experience and to tell others of the power of your name.

Maureen Sutton, Chester diocese, England

July 4th – Samual Azarah, bishop 1945
Reaching out

We remember before you now those known to us who are hurting but are not able to accept you as their loving heavenly Father. We ask that by the power of your Holy Spirit they will be aware of your longing to reach them and that they may reach out to you.

Canterbury diocese, England

July 5th – Martha of La Cambre, religious 13th century
Being Christian women

Thank you, Father, for the opportunity of being Christian women. Strengthen our belief in you. Sanctify us and grant us your love, patience, knowledge and wisdom to share Christ with our neighbours, even those we find difficult. At the end of our sojourn here on this earth, may we inherit your heavenly kingdom, through Christ, our Redeemer.

Mrs R. A. Gbadeyan, Kwara diocese, Nigeria

July 6th – Thomas More, martyr 1535
Sharing our faith

Dear God, as we try to worship you, help us through your
Spirit to be aware of opportunities to share the knowledge
of your love with those we meet each day. Grant us the
sensitivity to know when to speak and when to be silent,
and above all to show forth your glory. Through Jesus
Christ, our Lord.

   St Asaph diocese, Wales

July 7th – Joanna de Rampale, religious 1636
She does not share my faith

God of love,
she does not share my love for you, she does not know
   the freedom that comes from trusting in you:
   the freedom from fear,
   the freedom to abandon all cares and anxieties into
   your hands;
she does not know
   the peace and serenity of your presence,
   the assurance of your divine love;
she tolerates my 'religious' activities.

Lord, whether or not she accepts you is between you and
   her.
Grant that my love for you will not be a threat to her.
Grant me the wisdom to live and love so that she will
want to share my knowledge and faith in you.
One day, dear God, may we walk with you together.

   Joined in Love, New Zealand

July 8th – Priscilla, 1st century
For husbands

God of heaven, we thank you for the love we find in
marriage; we thank you for each gift you give. We pray to
you, Lord, for some of our husbands – though they go to
church for prayers and hear the preaching, yet they don't
forget their old ways of asking or believing in their older
gods. Father in heaven, we wives know for ourselves that
there are no other gods beside you. Send your Holy Spirit
through your people to the hearts of unbelieving
husbands so that their eyes may open to confess their sins
to you, so they believe in you only, and so that we, their
wives, may share your joy with them. Through Christ,
our Saviour.

Yunice Naamina, Maridi diocese, Sudan

July 9th – Veronica Guilani, religious 1727
Nagging wives

Many years ago, I decided that when I was married I was
definitely not going to be a nagging wife. The other day I
listened to myself talking to my husband and I realized
with horror that was just what I was doing . . . . .
nagging, niggling, needling. I decided to see if the Bible
has anything to say on this subject – yes, it never fails.
There were quite a few comments in Proverbs. Here are
some from *The Living Bible*.

'It is better to live in the corner of an attic than with a
crabby woman in a lovely home.' (21:9)

'. . . and a nagging wife annoys like constant dripping.'
(19:13)

'A constant dripping on a rainy day and a cranky
woman are much alike.'(28:15)

The message is clear, Lord. Stop nagging or be a drip.
Help me.
   Mainly Prayers, MU Young Families' department,
   United Kingdom

July 10th – Amalberga of Munsterbilzen c.772
For parents and children

Blessed Trinity, we confess that we often take for granted
the joys and difficulties of parenthood. We thank you for
the responsibilities of parenthood.

   Holy Father, we often forget that what seems so great a
load to carry is best carried with you as captain.

   Holy Jesus, may we always remember your great
sacrifice for us and all men, which cannot be compared
with what we have to make.

   Holy Spirit, assist us to instill the fear of God, the
Good News of salvation in our children and all around
us. Instruct us what to do in all situations: in joy and
anxieties; in frustration and near despair. Keep us strong
in you, and knit us in your love.

   In Jesus' precious name we pray.
   Ebun Carr, Gambia diocese, The Gambia

July 11th – Benedict, abbot c.540
For suffering women

Heavenly Father, we thank you for your love to all people,
especially when you gave us your only Son, Jesus Christ,
to come and demonstrate your love to us. You always
want all your people to be free but, Father, we pray to you
to break the strength and chains of the power of evil from
your people, especially the women with children who are
suffering. Many are homeless when they are pregnant; the
men refuse responsibility. Many don't have any kind of

income. Look down in mercy on them, give them the best solution to their suffering. Let them look at you for help; let them seek for your heavenly grace in their suffering.

We pray all this through Jesus Christ, our Lord.

Revd Sesai Tibikaraho, Bunyoro-Kitara diocese, Uganda

July 12th – *Veronica 1st century*
A Celtic prayer for a harassed mother

Lord, my day is too long. I am weary. My laden clothesline breaks. My baby cries, my children fight, my patience is nearly gone.

Nain* in her chimney corner says, 'Take a minute to wash your face – you will feel better and make a fresh start.'

Lord Jesus, wash me with living water, wash away my weariness and my impatience. Rock my babe with your love, quieten my children with your peace. Bless Nain, for she is near to you.

Jesus, Son of Mary's home, stay in our home with us today.

Barbara Sowood, Bangor diocese, Wales

* *'Nain' is 'Grandmother' in Welsh*

July 13th – *Silas, companion of Paul*
Continuing marriage

Lord, help us to remember when we first met and the strong love that grew between us. Help us to work that love into practical things so nothing can divide us. We ask for words both loving and kind, and for hearts always ready to ask forgiveness as well as to forgive.

Dear Lord, we put our marriage into your hands.

Ann Fry, Gloucester diocese, England

July 14th – *Reinofre of Brabant, recluse 650*

A battered wife

Ladies – you found the courage to start a new life,
don't go back to being a beaten wife.
Think of the children all you can,
we can make it without a man.
For God will be with you all the time,
He knows that your man has committed a crime.
It will be hard, on your own,
but just remember you're not alone.
All you ladies, do your best,
for God will help you start afresh.
Selina, St Albans diocese, England

July 15th – Swithun, bishop c.862
For those who cannot leave their homes

Heavenly Father, we pray that you may help those who
cannot leave their homes due to certain circumstances.
You are the most powerful God and you know the
innermost thoughts of every individual and the health of
every person. May you kindly use your powers to break
the bondage and the chains of evil which stop some of
your people from leaving their homes.

Enlighten their eyes so that they may see the Calvary
where our burdens were lifted. Help those who are unable
to walk also to glorify your name from where they are.
Give them all knowledge, courage and guidance to the
way which leads to eternity. In Jesus' name we pray.
Mugisha Hope, Muhabura diocese, Uganda

July 16th – Henry Williams, missionary 1867
For abused children

Dear Lord, we pray for all those children who see only the evil side of adult behaviour and who never receive the love that can heal their hurts. We lift to you the children whose homes do not provide them with a safe haven from which to go out into the world with confidence; the children who are cold or hungry; those who have no toys or books to stimulate their minds and imaginations; those who have nowhere to play, or who have to do adult work and have no time to play; those who are physically and mentally abused by the very people entrusted to care for them; and all those children who never hear of you and your love for them.

We pray that as you welcomed the children to you in earthly life, so you will enfold all children in your loving arms and keep them in your care.

Linda Hall, London diocese, England

July 17th – William White, bishop 1836
For single parents

O Lord, our God, we pray at this time for all single parents. We pray for those who have lost their spouse that, Lord, you will support them and help them bear the burden of raising their children which hitherto has been undertaken by two.

Concerning those who are in this position by reason of being victims of rape or any other form of sexual harassment, we pray Lord, that you uphold them emotionally and mentally. Let them receive love and understanding from fellow men and women and not feel ostracized or neglected.

We pray for those who are single parents by reason of

promiscuity or moral laxity, that you will have mercy and forgive them. Give them a repentant heart that they may return to you.

We pray for all the children in these various situations that you will be their guide and help. Lead them in the path of righteousness and truth, and help them to grow up to be a source of blessing to themselves and their various communities and nations.

We ask all these in the name of Jesus Christ, our Redeemer.

Dr S. O. Maloma, Kwara diocese, Nigeria

July 18th – Symphorosa of Tivoli c.130
Out into the unknown

O God, our heavenly Father, we pray that as we step out into the unknown, the light of the Holy Spirit may lead us to the place where we are needed most. We pray that we may reflect that light so that others too may reflect it, until the day when the whole world will be on fire for you.

We pray that we may never tire of following that light until at last it leads us to your eternal kingdom. Through Jesus Christ, our Lord.

St Asaph diocese, Wales

July 19th – Macrina c.379
Those leaving school

We pray for the rising generation and those who are preparing to leave school. Lord of all life, we pray that as the young people in each new generation discover your world in their own way, their energies may be used creatively in your service and their choices based on what is true and of real value.

Make plain your living word, that young people may grow in the faith of Christ to love and honour your name and to render service to others. For the vision of youth – its love of justice, strength of purpose and honesty of mind – we give you thanks and praise, dear Lord.

Nan Deedes, Winchester diocese, England

July 20th – *Margaret of Antioch 3rd century*
For the unemployed

Heavenly Father, we commend to your loving care all who are now suffering distress through unemployment. Strengthen and support them in their ordeal. Inspire and guide those in authority whose job it is to help them. Enable us to be sensitive to the needs of any known to us, and may we be ready to help where necessary.

In the name of Jesus Christ, our Lord.

Freda Howes, Winchester diocese, England

July 21st – *Angelina of Marsciano, religious 1435*
Families in adversity

Despite our hopes and efforts, Lord, we fail and things go wrong. We offer you the mistakes we have made in ourselves and in our marriages and families. We pray for people who are suffering now either from their own mistakes or from the mistakes of others:
for children separated from one parent and cut off from grandparents;
for parents who see their children for only part of the week;
for families who have many problems and lack hope;
for husbands and wives who no longer find joy in each other, who feel wounded and disillusioned, as their marriage breaks up;

for families who face death, illness, or disablement and
feel they cannot cope;
for the unemployed who feel hopeless and unwanted.
We hold them before you, Lord, for your healing love.
  *Christine McMullen, MU Anthology of Public Prayers,
  United Kingdom*

July 22nd – ST MARY MAGDALEN
For understanding

I'm hurt, Lord.
Please take my pain
and turn it into
understanding and love
for the one who hurt me.
  Rochester diocese, England

July 23rd – John Cassian, abbot c.360–435
Inner storms

Lord, be at the very centre of our being, we pray, so that
resting in your unending love we may weather our inner
storms and be channels of your peace.
  Salisbury diocese, England

July 24th – Thomas à Kempis, priest 1471
Prayer on the use of the tongue

Our Father and our God, we ask for forgiveness of sins
which we have committed against you – everliving God –
and our fellow men since our youth, through the use of
our tongues. Lord Jesus Christ, send your Holy Spirit
into our hearts to henceforth direct our tongues at all
times.
  We pray to you, O Lord, that when the last trumpet
shall sound, let not our tongues hinder us from entering

your rest in your eternal kingdom.

This is our plea in the name of Jesus Christ, our Lord.

Mrs J. F. Ibimodi, Kwara diocese, Nigeria

July 25th – ST JAMES THE APOSTLE
A busy woman's prayer

My Lord Jesus, as the pressures of my life throng about me I come to you for peace. My concerns crowd about me, jostling and bumping, pushing for attention, demanding action and my precious time.

But first, dear Lord, let me reach out and just touch the hem of your robe – still for a moment, caught by your gaze. You know my needs without words but what a relief to pour it all out and give them to you. I claim your peace, won for me at Calvary; your strength for the day.

Thank you for loving me so much. Send me out now into your world, ready to share your love. For your sake alone.

Birmingham diocese, England

July 26th – Anne, mother of the Blessed Virgin Mary
Grandchildren

Dear Father God, we thank you for the blessing of grandchildren; for babies who grow into lively active toddlers and teenagers; for all the joys and heartaches we suffer with them as they walk, run, learn, take exams, go to work or travel to far countries. We know they are upheld in your great love with all creation.

Please help us to remember all the children of the world; those who are hungry, sick, sad, lonely or frightened. May we work to alleviate their sufferings and show them your love.

Help us to be sensitive to those who are unable to have

children of their own and to be ever mindful of your great blessings.

This we ask in Jesus' name.
Rochester diocese, England

July 27th – William Huntingdon, priest 1909
For women's groups

O God, we pray for all the women's groups in our country. We pray that they may work in unity and harmony and support each other through meetings, work and prayer. Let them realize their goals, which are to bring happiness and peace to the women. We pray for their leaders that they may put you first and be guided by you to lead their fellow women. We pray through Christ, our Lord.

Four women from Kigezi diocese, Uganda

July 28th – Mary and Martha
The Mary and Martha prayer

Lord, there are Mothers' Union and women's group members who are good leaders; those with outstanding gifts to speak and make decisions; those who are good listeners, and those who quietly care; those whose work is little noticed, but without which our branch or group would be the poorer. Take all our gifts, Lord, and use them for your glory.

Margaret Wilson, MU Anthology of Public Prayers, United Kingdom

July 29th – William Wilberforce, social reformer 1833
Generous help

Father, may we never count the cost of helping and supporting those who need us. Make us willing and generous in our service, whether in deed or word, to help relieve the distress of others. Help us to bear one another's burdens and so fulfil the law of Christ. May your world be transformed from one of struggle and suffering to one of joy, peace and love.

Portsmouth diocese, England

July 30th – Julitta of Caesarea, martyr c.303
Hospitality

Heavenly Father, be with my husband and me in our home and in our hearts. May we always feel your presence with us. As you shared the home of your friends, Mary and Martha, in Bethany in the flesh, make us ever conscious that you are with us in spirit. When we are feeling tired and irritable help us to control our irritation and be watchful of our acts and words. Let home love be of the kind that never fails; no goodness and gentleness outside will atone for unlovingness and uncharitableness at home. Help us to be hospitable, and when friends, acquaintances or strangers enter our home may they feel the influence of two people trying to be good Christians and striving to be Christlike. These things we ask in the name of Jesus.

Bradford diocese, England

July 31st – Joseph of Arimathea
Daily doings

Grant, O Lord, that everyone who has to do with me this
day may be the happier for it. May it be given me,
moment by moment, what I should say; and may I have
the wisdom of a loving heart to say the right thing rightly.
Keep me alive to the feelings of others; give me the quick
eye for little kindnesses, that I may be ready in doing
them and gracious in receiving them. Give me a quick
perception of the needs of others and may I be eager-
hearted in helping them. For Christ, my Saviour's sake.

Mary Pritchard, Gloucester diocese, England

AUGUST

Rest and Recreation

August 1st – Sophia of Rome, martyr c.120
For those travelling

O God, our Father in heaven, thank you because you are omnipresent. In your great mercy, protect all travellers all over the world. Guide all those who travel by air, road, water, rail and even those who journey on foot. Take control of all their vessels and vehicles, as well as the routes through which they will pass. In Jesus Christ, our Saviour's name, we pray.

Mrs R. A. Gbadeyan, Kwara diocese, Nigeria

August 2nd – Etheldritha, religious c.835
Before driving

Dear Lord, may I cause annoyance, anxiety, injury or bereavement to no one, and please help all other drivers to do the same. May all of us who use our roads be courteous and considerate. Save us from the momentary wrong decision and from lack of concentration. Deter those who would drive recklessly.

Guide and inspire all who make and maintain our vehicles and those who design our roads and control the traffic. May all who travel on our roads be able to do so safely and with peace of mind.

I ask for the good of all mankind, through our only advocate and mediator, our Saviour, Jesus Christ.

Freda Redfearn, London diocese, England

August 3rd – Germanus of Auxerre, bishop 5th century
Life's road

Holy Father, take me by the hand and lead me along life's road.

Blessed Jesus, Son of the Father, find me when I lose the way and bring me back to God.

Loving Spirit, gift of the Father and the Son, be my refreshment on the journey and the light which guides my path.

Glorious Trinity – Father, Son and Holy Spirit – be my destination, that when my travels are over I may find my rest in you at journey's end.

Carlisle diocese, England

August 4th – John Vianney, priest and pastor 1859
Ears pierced

Dear heavenly Father, I am feeling frightened because I am having my ears pierced soon. I am frightened that it will hurt so please make me think that it won't.

Laura Hagger (aged 7), London diocese, England

August 5th – Oswald of Northumbria, martyr 642
My cat

Dear God, please make my cat's toe better, because she is my best friend in the world. Thank you.

Roxanne Jones (aged 6), London diocese, England

August 6th – THE TRANSFIGURATION OF OUR LORD
My God, I am trusting in you

My God, now and always I am trusting in you. As the sun and the air, the soil and the rain nourish the summer rose, so I feel peace and health, strength and control flowing through me.

' For these bountiful gifts of your goodness to take and to share, I thank you, Lord.
I am revitalized.
I am filled with God.
I can do all things through Jesus Christ.

George diocese, South Africa

August 7th – John Mason Neale, priest 1866
We have time to enjoy each other

Loving creator, it seems as though you've given us a
second chance. After all these years of busy-ness, of
deadlines, of demands, of other's concerns; now, in our
retirement, at last we have time with each other.
We can enjoy the privilege of planning each day – guide
us as we plan.
We can relax and take outings together – restore us in
these times.
We can take up new hobbies and new interests – be near
us as we choose.
May our retirement be a time of re-creation, and in all we
do may we know your presence with us, your love
surrounding us to eternity.

   Joined in Love, New Zealand

August 8th – Dominic, friar and priest 1221
A Mothers' Union aid to prayer

Make time for God
Obey His word
Trust in His promises and forgive
Here in me is where love starts
Endeavour to be of good cheer at all times
Rest in Him, His peace will comfort you
Strengthen others and test your faith

Use your talents – we all have them
New life in Jesus every day
Imagination in prayer deepens understanding
Offer friendship – we all need it
Never lose heart – even when all seems lost
   Sheffield diocese, England

August 9th – Mary Sumner, founder of MU 1828–1921
Mary Sumner's personal prayer

All this day, O Lord, let me touch as many lives as
possible for thee; and every life I touch, do thou by thy
Spirit quicken, whether through the word I speak, the
prayer I breathe, or the life I live.

MU Anthology of Public Prayers, United Kingdom

August 10th – Laurence, deacon and martyr 258
Serving others

Dear Lord and heavenly Father, let not our lips be silent
when others need our service, nor our hands be idle when
they ask our aid. Let not our hearts be closed when others
seek our love. May our minds be alert when our counsel
is asked for.

Our hearts are yours, O Lord. May our praise and
thanksgiving to you be in our service to others.

Susie M. Payne, Worcester diocese, England

August 11th – Clare of Assisi, abbess 1253
Outcasts of society

Lord Jesus, you cared for the outcasts of society. We know
it is easy to care for those we like; give us something of
your compassion for the unmentionables of our society –
the alcoholic, the addict, the poor – those who we would
like to sweep under the carpet, and pretend that they
don't exist.

Open our eyes that we might see beneath present
circumstances; open our ears that we can hear your voice
guiding us; open our hearts to enfold all your children.

Help us never to be content or complacent while one of
our fellow human beings is in need of our help.

Rochester diocese, England

August 12th – Clara of Remiremont, abbess 7th century
God's hands and feet

Heavenly Father, your Son said to us, '. . . inasmuch as
you do it unto the least of these, you do it unto me'. Let
us remember as we go about our daily lives that we do all
things in your name.

We are your hands when we tend the sick, when we
comfort the bereaved, when we feed the hungry, teach the
children.

We are your feet when we visit those in need.

Lord, you have called us and consecrated us to be your
body here: your eyes and heart, hands and feet. Send your
Holy Spirit on us that we may do your will, knowing you
are always with us, whatever you call us to do.

Eva Sparey, Gloucester diocese, England

August 13th – Jeremy Taylor, bishop and teacher 1667
Look up and laugh and live

O Lord, help us to show your loving kindness to all in this
world who may feel themselves little loved or forgotten,
and those to whom love has never come. In their
loneliness, help us to cheer them, that they may meet all
life's ills with gallant and high-hearted happiness.

Let them know that you do, always, love them.

Lord, I would look up and love and laugh and live!

St Asaph diocese, Wales

August 14th – Maximilian Kolbe, priest and martyr 1941
Concern for our neighbours

God, our Father, we thank and praise you for our
neighbours. We are grateful to you for having them in our
neighbourhood. But we know that we do not show them
enough love according to your teaching.

We do not have enough time to talk to them,
we do not have enough time to visit them,
we also do not intervene in their problems.
Lord, give us courage to take your love to them. Being in a
hurry or very tired or not having something to give them,
very often we do not listen to them when they approach
us. O Lord, give us wisdom to show to them your love in
practice so that they may know your salvation.

We trust in you, Lord.

Byumba diocese, Rwanda

August 15th – Mary, mother of Jesus
A prayer for parents

Heavenly Father, you made men and women to be
partners and you gave them love. When they have their
children, allow them to thank you. Give them your love to
care for their children, and open their eyes to understand
your gifts. In the name of our Saviour, Jesus Christ.

Mrs N. Gbarago Masewungu, Maridi diocese, Sudan

August 16th – Holy women of the Old Testament
For personal relationships

O God, our creator and Father, we thank you for making
men and women in your image. We enjoy being with you
in worship, and we are glad that by your guidance and
with your grace we can find delight and enrichment in
each other. Help us, this day, to understand a little more
of the mystery of our nature and of the relationship of
men and women.

We pray for boys and girls that they may develop
naturally in body, mind and spirit.

We pray for teenagers: help them to grow in love and

understanding, and to treat themselves and others with respect.

We pray for those who are married: help them to go on growing in love and understanding. Where there are difficulties, show them how to overcome them. Where there is failure, assure them of Christian forgiveness and of grace for the future.

We pray for those who are bringing up their families alone: may human friendship enrich their lives, and service bring them fulfilment. Through Jesus Christ, our Lord.

MU Service Book, United Kingdom

August 17th – Barbara Heck, Methodist missionary 1804
Taking exams and finding jobs

In the beginning, God told Adam after sinning that he had to work hard all his life in order to produce enough food for himself. This was a curse on the ground from God, and so we too must work hard. There are so many different kinds of jobs people are doing; some are still training for certain jobs, some still have to do exams. This has caused people to be anxious and to worry but, Father, we thank you for your promise that you will care for us if we cast our worries and anxieties on you. You continued to show us how much you cared for us when you compared us with birds and flowers which do not care about what they will eat or wear tomorrow – we know that you love us more than you love any of these. Help us, Lord, to rest assured that you will provide for our needs in every way if we only lean against you and rely on you for everything. In Jesus Christ we pray.

Four women from Kigezi diocese, Uganda

August 18th – William DuBose, priest 1918
For teenagers

Our heavenly Father, creator of all mankind, we
remember and pray for all teenagers. We recognize that
the teenage period is fraught with strain and stress:
mentally, physically, emotionally and spiritually.
Therefore we ask, Lord, that you grant all our teenagers
your peace, courage, confidence and wisdom as they seek
to understand themselves and the world around them,
that they do not go astray.

We pray for all those who lead and instruct them, that
you endow them with the understanding and wherewithal
to lead and teach them aright, that these young people
may find their true selves in you.

All these we ask of you through Jesus Christ, our
Lord.

Dr S. O. Malomo, Kwara diocese, Nigeria

August 19th – Caritas Pirckheimer, abbess 1532
Lifestyle

Dear Lord, help me to develop a lifestyle that reflects the
fact that I'm only a temporary camper here on earth; that
my true home is in heaven.

Peterborough diocese, England

August 20th – Bernard of Clairvaux, abbot 1153
For those going astray

Our heavenly Father, we pray for teenagers who are
particularly troublesome and tending towards delinquency
that, Lord, you will prevent and halt them from plunging
into evil. We also remember all those who are in Remand
homes or custody, that you send your Holy Spirit to
minister to their hearts and convert them so that they may

truly repent and turn to you. All these we ask of you through Jesus Christ, our Lord.

Dr S. O. Malomo, Kwara diocese, Nigeria

August 21st – Humbelina, abbess 1141
It all came right today

Thank you, loving God, for guiding us through this difficult time in our lives; for being always with us, even when we felt it hard to find your presence.

Today it has all come right and we are joyful in the knowledge that our hopes and prayers have been answered in your way.

We rededicate our lives to you in service, confirmed and strengthened in our faith, in the name of Jesus.

George diocese, South Africa

August 22nd – Marguerite Andre, religious 1645
A prayer for young people

We come to you, Father, as we have sons and daughters in their youth. Some are safeguarded by the blood of Jesus but many are going as they wish and are exposed to all evils. Father, we are in an area in danger from HIV/AIDS; our youth are threatened, the parents have no hope but worries, we are not sure of continuity. Many problems are facing the home and other places of the youth.

Bring them to you, O Lord; with your loving kindness make them yours. Father, open their ears and hearts to understand your word so that they can think, speak and act in accordance with your will. Through Jesus Christ, our Lord.

Revd Sesai Tibikaraho, Bunyoro-Kitara diocese, Uganda

August 23rd – Rose of Lima, mystic 1617
AIDS

We pray for those who are already victims of AIDS, that they may not be led into despair but instead draw nearer to you, commit their lives into your loving hands and know your loving care. We pray for the many orphans who are left behind by the victims of AIDS, that they may have hope in you and trust that you will be all in all for them. We pray this in the name of our Father, Son and Holy Spirit.

Marion Sebuhinja, Muhabura diocese, Uganda

August 24th – ST BARTHOLOMEW THE APOSTLE
For healing

Lord Jesus Christ, we ask you to be with all those who need your healing touch today. Come in all your power and surround them with your love. Bless the work of our hospitals, health centres, day centres, the hospice movement, the Samaritans and all those who seek to ease the pain and anxieties of the sick.

Julie Densham, Bristol diocese, England

August 25th – Gregory of Utrecht, missionary c.707–775
For troubled homes

Lord, ... is so unhappy today, full of anxieties and frightened about tomorrow. Send your calm and steadfast love to them – let the family know that you are with them. Enfold them in your loving arms until the hurt, the anger, the bitterness and hate eases, and show them that there is a path to the light through darkness.

Brenda Thorpe, York diocese, England

August 26th – Teresa Jornet Ibars, religious 1897
Half an hour of peace

Half an hour of peace, Lord, is it too much to ask?
as my blood pressure pounds through task after task.
I'm so tired of being good, Lord, and cooking this, and
cleaning that;
with time spent solving squabbles; I've even had to scold
the cat.
Just a half hour's peace, Lord! with no one else in sight.
Yes, that would give me sustenance and see me through
this plight.
Half an hour spent with you amid demanding toils or
strife,
restoring sanity and calm to my disordered, hectic life.

   *Carol Booth, Mainly Prayers, MU Young Families
department, United Kingdom*

*August 27th – Caesarius, bishop, and Caesaria, abbess,
6th century*
Prayer for a lost son

Lord Jesus, thank you for your word in the Bible that
gives me hope. I pray to you for all children who have
gone astray, that you will bring them back to the fold and
bless them and lead them aright.

   This, my son, in particular has gone off the track. You
alone know where he is. Draw him out of the net he has
entangled himself in and save him, for your name's sake.

   A desperate mother, Bo diocese, Sierra Leone

August 28th – Augustine of Hippo 430
For serenity

Slow me down, Lord, ease the pounding of my heart by
the quietening of my mind. Steady my hurried pace with
the vision of the eternal reach of time. Give me amid the
confusion of my day the calmness of the everlasting hills.
Inspire me to send my roots deep into the soil of life's
enduring values, that I may grow towards the stars of my
greater destiny.

N. H., London diocese, England

August 29th – Beheading of John the Baptist
Awareness of others

Heavenly Father, whoever we are and in whatever
situation we find ourselves, we have an effect on the lives
of other people and they have an effect on us. We pray
that we may always be sensitive to their feelings and never
be so caught up in our own lives and problems that we
cannot spare time to listen to and talk with them.

We thank you for all those people who touch our lives
and give us an example to follow. Forgive us for those
times when we have not got on with others through our
own fault.

Above all, may we always be filled with the love of your
Son, Jesus Christ, our Lord.

Chelmsford diocese, England

August 30th – Robert McDonald, priest 1913
Travel

Heavenly Father, we thank you for holidays, for times of
rest and relaxation, and for opportunities to travel.

Protect all travellers, whether by sea or by land or in the

air. May they return refreshed in body, mind and spirit.
    We ask this in your name.
    Rochester diocese, England

August 31st – John Bunyan, author 1688
Be with us, Lord

Be with us, Lord, through all the burdens and heat of the
day, so that as night comes upon us we may find your
grace within our hearts; your blessing on our work; your
mercy on our living; and your light upon our faces as we
turn homewards in our last hour through the gate of
death to life eternal.
    Revd Sister Hazel Smith, St Albans diocese, England

SEPTEMBER

Harvest

September 1st – Giles of Provence, hermit c. 710
The seasons

Dear Lord Jesus, we thank you for the seasons of the year.
For spring and the flowers it brings with it, and the fresh
green grass.
For summer with the bright yellow sun and the bright
green leaves hanging from the trees.
For autumn and the crunchy green apples and the golden
harvest.
And last of all for winter and the white snow, whiter than
milk.
We thank you, Lord.

   Kim Morton (aged 10), Exeter diocese, England

September 2nd – Martyrs of Papua New Guinea 1942
For women who suffer

Lord Jesus Christ, you told the women of Jerusalem not to
weep for you but to weep for themselves.
Be with the women of . . . . . as they suffer violence in
their homes; as they weep for their sons, caught up in the
violence.
Be with the women and children of . . . . . , trapped in
prostitution by poverty.
Be with the women in . . . . . who live with domestic
violence, who have learnt not to weep for their own pains,
who have suffered so long they are numb.
Strengthen your Church in its care and support of all who
are in pain.
Help us all to be sensitive and caring, for you are the Lord
who suffers and serves.

   Province of Papua New Guinea

September 3rd – Cuthberga, religious, c.725
Using gifts

God the Holy Spirit, Lord of heaven and earth, we
acknowledge your goodness in giving to your people gifts
to be used in the service of your kingdom.
Grant us, we pray, the wisdom to identify those gifts
which you have given us, and the courage and sensitivity
to use them creatively for the good of our fellow human
beings and for the glory of your name.

Coventry diocese, England

*September 4th – Albert Schweitzer, medical missionary
and theologian 1965*
Prayer for healing

Let me weep your tears, Jesus; your compassion freely show.
Make me humble in your service; let the Holy Spirit flow
in the healing of the suffering, in the binding of the soul,
in the gathering of the fragments needed, Lord, to make
one whole.
Praises be to God the Father, to the Spirit and the Son.
Thank you, thank you, precious Jesus, for the mercy you
have shown
in the healing of the suffering, in the binding of the soul,
in the gathering of the fragments needed, Lord, to make
one whole.

Morwen Pippen, Monmouth diocese, Wales

September 5th – Angela Hughes, religious 1866
Prayer for today

Lord, I am praying for today because the rest of eternity
begins here. Yesterday is beyond recall, tomorrow is
beyond comprehension, but today I want to serve you
well.

I will meet many people today – help me to turn their thoughts to you by my reactions, by my attitude to life, by my words, and by the expression on my face.

I will meet many situations today – help me to be patient, humble, calm and resourceful.

I will perform many tasks today – help me to be diligent, cheerful and economical in my use of time.

But above all, may my mind be constantly directed to you today so that I may look back tonight on a day which we have spent together.

Salisbury diocese, England

September 6th – Charles Fox, missionary 1977
Intercession

Lord, our God, may your peace shine among us, may your love set us free. May the leaders of the nations seek the way that leads to peace and may human rights everywhere be respected. Teach us to recognize your presence in every person, and above all, in those who suffer. Teach those who have plenty to share the fruits of the earth among all peoples. Father, your kingdom come.

Edinburgh diocese, Scotland

September 7th – Saints and Martyrs of the Pacific
Thank you for this moment

Loving Creator, thank you for this moment, when I know your presence, feel your hand guiding my actions and my planning, making me ready for new opportunities and new tasks.

Thank you for your presence with me.

Joined in Love, New Zealand

September 8th – BIRTH OF THE BLESSED VIRGIN MARY

New baby

O God, thank you for the joy of a new baby in our family, for a new life which is part of us and yet a separate being. As we love and care for our child help us to teach him/her to know and love you as his/her friend.

Chelmsford diocese, England

September 9th – Kieran of Clonmacnois, abbot c. 516-549

After a miscarriage

O Lord, there are some women who are crying for not having children; some of them have had an accident or had an abortion. They badly need children; they do not show their sorrow to everybody but their hearts are burning with that desire. Help them, Lord, hear their cry. Change their sorrow into happiness. O Lord, listen to our prayers.

Byumba diocese, Rwanda

September 10th – Edmund Peck, missionary 1924

Handicapped baby

Loving Jesus, our Saviour, you who always had compassion for all that were sick and suffering who came to you, we pray in your name for all babies that are handicapped physically or mentally, all over the world.

In particular we pray for . . . . . In their helplessness, O Lord, we pray that you will send your divine help to them. Grant to those who need love and care people who will provide them. As they face a future which to us looks bleak and difficult, Lord, help them to overcome those obstacles which may prevent them from living the fulfilling life which you have purposed for them. We thank you for all those who in one way or another help to relieve their suffering; that, Lord, you will bless them abundantly and make them relentless in their good works.

Dr S. O. Malomo, Kwara diocese, Nigeria

September 11th – Deiniol, bishop 6th century
A stillborn child

O Lord, I felt such terrible disappointment and sadness when they told me my baby had died. I felt so different from all the other mothers. He had been part of my body for all those months, and now he is gone. I wanted to hold him, to feel his warm body in my arms. I wanted to love him. I never had a chance to tell him how much I loved him. I have only cried for him, missing him.

And then I thought of you Lord. I knew he was safe with you. You will love him in such a special way, you will care for him in your heaven. I feel he is safe, Lord. I still miss him, and sometimes when I am alone I cry for him and long for him. But that terrible loneliness is not there when I think that he is at home with you.

Ann Murphy, Llandaff diocese, Wales

September 12th – John Henry Hobart, bishop 1830
Starting school

It was heart-wrenching, Lord, her first day at school. How would she manage without me? Would she still be crying when I collected her at the end of the day?

But when she ran to meet me, chattering happily about her day, it was humbling to realize that she was moving away from her dependency on me.

It was frustrating, Lord, having to stand on the sidelines, watching her fight her battles, make her mistakes – wanting so desperately to step in and help but knowing that she would not welcome interference.

Lord, it's hard being a mother – so many conflicting emotions: joy, apprehension, pain, sadness, frustration, anger. But, Lord, it is a very special task which you have set me. Thank you for the privilege, and the knowledge that you are constantly with me to uphold and strengthen, to comfort and grieve with me, to share my joys. Thank you, Lord.

Rochester diocese, England

September 13th – Cyprian, bishop and martyr 258
For senior secondary schools

Almighty God, we pray for our institutions of learning in all countries; more particularly, we pray for secondary schools. We commit to your care all boys, girls and teachers in these institutions so that evil may have no room in the hearts of these youngsters. We pray that the Good News of salvation may reach them and that a spiritual revival may take root in their lives. We thank you, Lord, for those who have already received you. Control their lives that they may witness for you; use them for your service to bring many others to you.

Lord, we pray for your healing power for those who have broken spirits, or are worried or spiritually malnourished. Make our ministry a source of blessing for them and give us the ability, the resources, the time and the love to minister to them. Through Jesus Christ, our Lord.

Joy Shalita, Muhabura diocese, Uganda

September 14th – Holy Cross Day
The prayer of the chalice

> Father, to you I raise my whole being,
> A vessel emptied of self. Accept, Lord,
> this my emptiness, and so fill me with
> yourself – your light, love, and life –
> that these your precious gifts may
> radiate through me, and overflow
> the chalice of my heart into
> the hearts of all with
> whom I come into
> contact this day,
> revealing to
> them the beauty
> of your joy and
> wholeness,
> and
> the
> serenity
> of your peace,
> which nothing can destroy.

Frances Nuttal, Oxford diocese, England

September 15th – Mary at the cross
Sudden death

Everlasting God, we thank you for sending Jesus Christ to
open the gate to you, as we will all come to you through
death. I pray you to allow us not to meet sudden death –
it breaks the hearts of parents and friends. Lord, our
Father, guide us all when we are in danger. I pray through
Christ, our Lord.

Agnes Amona, Maridi diocese, Sudan

September 16th – Ninian of Galloway, bishop and missionary c 432
Reaping the harvest

Abba Father, you have shown your great love by sending Jesus into the world to give new life to all people. Pour your Spirit on the Church that it may preach the Gospel to all in every place.

Call out men and women to reap the harvest fields here in our country and beyond our shores. May they see with the eyes of faith the kingdom in our midst, and reach forward in courage and hope to the kingdom that is to come.

Edinburgh diocese, Scotland

September 17th – Hildegard of Bingen, mystic 1179
Decade of Evangelism

O Lord God, our heavenly Father, we thank you for the many gifts you have bestowed on us. Especially we thank you for your Son, our Lord Jesus Christ, who by His life and death showed us the way of love by which we come to you.

We thank you, too, for the gift of your Holy Spirit, who dwelling within us kindles such a flame in our hearts that as the spark runs through the stubble we may be enabled by His power to spread the joy of loving you.

St Asaph diocese, Wales

September 18th – Founders, benefactors and missionaries of the Church of Canada
A prayer from the Canadian Mothers' Union

Loving Father, we thank you for calling us to be members of the Mothers' Union. We praise your name, and the knowledge that you have drawn us closer to you through prayer, study, fellowship and service. Thank you, that by your grace we can do all of these things.

Forgive us, Father, for the times we have not remained close to you. We are acutely aware of how little fruit from our ministry we offer you. We know and accept your promise to answer our prayers, so we now ask your blessing on the members of the Mothers' Union. Fill us with your Spirit to empower us for your service and guide us where you would have us grow. Show us where we can put our faith into action.

We thank you, Father, for filling us with your Spirit. We know you are changing our lives in spirit, mind and body. Our hearts overflow with joy that you are making us 'perfect and complete, lacking in nothing', because it means that your kingdom is being extended and your name glorified. Thank you, Father. Thank you, Jesus. Thank you, Spirit.

The Mothers' Union, Province of Canada

September 19th – Theodore of Canterbury, archbishop 690
Starved of friendship

Father, I bring to you in prayer people whose lives are starved of friendship: those who find it difficult to make friends; those who are cut off from their friends by distance; and those who in old age have lost the friends they had. Comfort and sustain them, O Lord, with your love.

Chelmsford diocese, England

September 20th – Saints and martyrs of Australia
A prayer from Australia

God our Father, source of all creation, we praise and thank
you for the beauty of this land in which we live. The
majesty of ancient, towering cliffs, snow-capped mountains,
rain-forest, coastline and desert speak to us of your
eternal power and glory. The rainbow-colours of birds in
flight and flowers blooming after desert rains remind us of
your covenant-promise given to Noah so long ago.

In the richness and variety of the gifts of our aboriginal
people, and of all those from many races who have settled
in this great southern land, we see the hope and challenge
of our future. Teach us to live together in love, peace and
acceptance of one another, so that our lives may witness
to the truth of your Gospel of salvation, and may the light
of the great southern cross shine as a beacon in your
world. In Jesus' name we pray.

The Mothers' Union in Australia

September 21st – ST MATTHEW THE APOSTLE
A just share

O Lord God, look in mercy on our sisters and brothers in the
developing nations, and grant them a just share in the gifts
you have given us all. Strengthen in them all that is good,
and give them discernment in adapting to the ways of others.

Look with mercy on the Church of your dear Son, here
in our land and around the world. Pour out anew the gifts
of the Spirit, and grant justice between the nations.

Call out men and women who will speak to the world,
across all barriers of language and culture, of your mighty
acts in Christ, to whom, with you and the Spirit, be all
honour and glory now and for ever.

Dorothy Corney, St Albans diocese, England

September 22nd – Salaberga, religious c.665
For the poor

Father of mercy, you created us for your own. We thank you, Father. You are full of love, you care for us in all ways.

Look down with mercy on all our situations; hear the cry of your people who have no shelter, no food, no basic needs. Forgive us and forgive them. Provide for them, Lord: you have given them responsibility for providing for others but they have nothing. Children are going naked, they are not having balanced diets, they are not going to school – they are not happy in such poverty.

The scripture tells us that if we ask from you through our Lord, Jesus Christ, you will give. We pray for all these, trusting in your word.

Revd Sesai Tibikaraho, Bunyoro-Kitara diocese, Uganda

September 23rd – Churchill Julius, archbishop 1938
In times of disaster

O Lord, Jesus Christ, we pray for all involved in . . . . . tragedy. May your love surround and your strength support them so that they may have faith and courage to endure. Give your compassion to all endeavouring to help them.

May your blessing rest upon the dying, the injured, and all who mourn their loved ones. We ask this for your dear sake.

MU Service Book, United Kingdom

September 24th – Thecla of Iconium, martyr 1st century
For refugees

Almighty God, the source of truth and peace, of comfort
and joy; we want to remember all those who need you for
their comfort, who need your peace and lack truth. We
ask, Lord, that you may look down from heaven on all
those in refugee camps, who are suffering and need you as
their comfort. We also place into your hands those
suffering in the world around us. Help them, O Lord
Jesus, to realize that you suffered here on earth for us and
paid the price for our sins so that we are assured of
eternal life. Let that console them, O Lord, that they may
learn to know that their suffering is just for a short time.
In your name we pray.

Four women from Kigezi diocese, Uganda

September 25th – Lancelot Andrewes, bishop 1626
Help us to be good neighbours

Father, help us to help each other; teach us to be willing
to do the small things just as gladly as those which are
important. Help us to be good neighbours; may our
words, our example and influence make life happier for
those around us.

Eunice Davies, St Albans diocese, England

September 26th – Sergius, abbot 1392
Consistent communion

Loving God, teach me that my prayer depends not on my
feelings nor on my efforts but rather on your consistent
communion with me. Hold the attentions of my mind and
spirit, and give me
not only words but songs,
not only familiar pictures but original paintings,

not only memories of happiness and sadness but tears of yearning and hope, that I may praise you with every member and breath of my whole being. In the name of Jesus, my King and my God.

Rochester diocese, England

September 27th – The martyrs of Melanesia
Jesus, the canoe

O Jesus, be the canoe that holds me up in the sea of life;
be the rudder that helps me in the straight road;
be the outrigger that supports me in times of temptation;
let your Spirit be my sail that carries me through each day.
Keep my body strong, so I can paddle steadfastly on in the voyage of life.

Province of Melanesia

September 28th – Lioba, abbess and missionary
c. 700-780
For women in positions of leadership

Lord Jesus, in whom all power and authority in heaven and on earth has been vested, we beseech you to grant to all women in various positions of authority and leadership, and in particular . . . . . who was recently appointed as . . . . . , the wisdom and strength to carry out their duties without fear or discrimination. Grant to them the enablement with which they will accomplish the task that is before them. We pray that as they combine these duties with other commitments they will not neglect one for the other but rather have greater achievements in all spheres of their endeavours to the glory of your name.

Dr S. O. Malomo, Kwara diocese, Nigeria

September 29th – ST MICHAEL AND ALL ANGELS
Call to ministry

O Lord, stir the hearts and minds of men and women today; give them your courage to step forth, take up the call and become ministers of your word to future generations; through Jesus Christ, our Lord.

Rochester diocese, England

September 30th – Jerome, priest and teacher 420
For the clergy and all who minister

O Holy Spirit, we pray that your voice may be heard by all who are needed for the service of God in His Church. Fill their hearts with grace to obey, and with humility to lead your children ever closer to your side. Show to them the spirit of true thankfulness for their calling and unwavering faith through all times of doubt or difficulty, that your will may be done on earth as in heaven.

MU Service Book, United Kingdom

OCTOBER

Coming to Maturity

October 1st – Marie-Joseph Aubert, social reformer 1926
Autumn thoughts

Gather me to you, Lord, like ripened apples.
Reap me and bind me like the sheaves of corn,
shape me and tidy me like garden hedges,
and all the useless trimmings burn.

Open my eyes to autumn's painful story:
the gold to grey, the stripping and the death.
The heart of this is Easter's radiant story,
when Christ will breathe in us his Spirit breath.

Farewell then to the summer's brilliant garden.
For the hey-day of my life accept my thanks.
Welcome to winter now, frost gleam and darkness.
To all that is in store for me, may I say yes.
Rochester diocese, England

*October 2nd – Anthony, Earl of Shaftesbury and
philanthropist 1885*
Discovery

O God, our heavenly Father, help us, as we travel the path
of discovery, to find you in our everyday lives and in the
wonder of creation. Open our hearts to the needs of
others; that strengthened by the Holy Spirit we may
continue to grow in understanding and love, through Jesus
Christ, our Lord.
*Sheila Hindmarch and Dena Gladwell, Portsmouth
diocese, England*

October 3rd – George Bell, bishop 1958
For peace

Lord, our heavenly Father, I pray for countries at war.
Send your Holy Spirit into the hearts of men. Allow them

to solve their problems in peace, Lord. Take the selfishness in their hearts away and send your Holy Spirit to guide their minds, through Christ, our Lord.

Yodita Elisa, Maridi diocese, Sudan

October 4th – Francis of Assisi, friar and deacon 1226
Our friends, the animals

Hear our humble prayer, O God, for our friends the animals, especially for animals that are suffering; for all that are overworked and underfed and cruelly treated; for all wistful creatures in captivity that beat against their bars; for any that are hunted or lost or deserted or frightened or hungry; for all that are in pain or dying; for all that must be put to death. We entreat for them all your mercy and pity; and for those who deal with them we ask a heart of compassion and gentle hands and kindly words. As for ourselves, make us true friends to animals and so share the blessing of the merciful. For the sake of your Son the tender-hearted, Jesus Christ, our Lord.

Gloucester diocese, England

October 5th – Maurus, monk 6th century
Dumb friends

Maker of earth and sea and sky,
creation's sovereign Lord and King,
who hung the starry worlds on high
and formed alike the sparrow's wing,
bless the dumb creatures in your care
and listen to their voiceless prayer.

Sheila King, Portsmouth diocese, England

October 6th – Saints and martyrs of Asia
For schools, colleges and universities

O Lord, our God, we pray for all those who are engaged
in education: all lecturers, teachers, tutors and students in
our schools, colleges and universities. Inspire them in
their studies to acknowledge and love the truth and enable
them with joy and patience to share it with others. Grant,
above all, that they may know that the fear of the Lord is
the beginning of wisdom.

MU Service Book, United Kingdom

*October 7th – William Tyndale, priest, translator and
martyr 1536*
Prayer for disappointed young people

Loving Father, where college doors remain closed to some
school-leavers, let other doors leading to a bright future
open. Grant the disappointed the vision to see the way
they should go and then, in the strength of the Holy
Spirit, the courage to take it.

Sheila Walker, Chelmsford diocese, England

October 8th – Birgitta of Sweden, mystic 1373
Growing up

O God, our heavenly Father, we pray for all young people
in the difficulties they face in their lives just 'growing up':
relationships between the sexes; study and examinations;
the choice of careers; leisure activities; the search for
employment. May we have insight, patience and love in
our dealings with them, and we ask your blessing upon
them as they pass through this new, exciting part of their
lives.

Chelmsford diocese, England

October 9th – Denys and his companions, martyrs 258
About to be married

Dear Lord, we thank you at all times for the wonderful
world around us and for the great gifts of sight, and
sound and understanding.

We ask you, especially at this time when . . . . . and
. . . . . are about to start their married life together, to
increase their awareness of each other's needs, so that
their home will be a place of happiness and love. May
they be strengthened in their love for you and in turn
share that love with others.

May your blessing be on them as they travel on life's
way, now and always.

St Edmundsbury and Ipswich diocese, England

October 10th – Paulinus, bishop and missionary 644
Mixed marriages

Lord Jesus, I've read in the Bible that in you there are no
differences in class, race or colour. So . . . . . and I come
to ask you to bless our marriage. We are from different
. . . . . (race, religion, denomination, culture) and we've
come feeling hurt from the rejection of others. But we've
come with our eyes wide open, knowing it will not always
be easy and that people will watch and wonder. May we
never take each other for granted. May we continue to
learn from each other's tradition and may our different
backgrounds bring new flavour and new richness into our
home. You are a God who is beyond limitations. You are
love and your love is without prejudice. May our marriage
reflect your love and your acceptance of us.

Joined in Love, New Zealand

October 11th – Philip the Deacon
For our married children

O Lord, Jesus Christ, we ask your blessing on our
children who are married. Grant them joy in their life
together and a love which grows deeper year by year. May
they rely upon your grace to guide and help them at all
times. We pray this for your sake.
  MU Service Book, United Kingdom

October 12th – Elizabeth Fry, prison reformer 1845
For sons- and daughters-in-law

Almighty God, you introduced the mystery that a man
and a woman should live together as husband and wife,
leaving their parents to become one. We thank you, Lord,
for your fatherly care and for making it possible for our
sons and daughters to marry. For as much as without you
we cannot do anything, we ask you to make their homes
full of peace and love. Bless them with good children.
Now that they have married their husbands and wives
they are our sons and daughters. Make us loving and
faithful fathers and mothers to our sons- and daughters-
in-law. Father, send your Holy Spirit into the hearts of our
sons- and daughters-in-law; and increase their love so that
they will accept us as fathers- and mothers-in-law, even as
their own mothers and fathers. Help us to be enduring,
understanding, merciful and kind; and to live together
peacefully in the name of our Lord, Jesus Christ.
  Hannah Aduke Haruma J.P., Kwara diocese, Nigeria

October 13th – Edward the Confessor, king 1066
For broken homes

Our heavenly Father, provider of love and peace to all
humanity, it is your will that we marry and build homes.
But, Lord, you have taught us that unless our homes are
built in you, we labour in vain without hope. We therefore
pray for those families with broken homes and broken
relationships.

Remind them, Lord Jesus, that you are the foundation
of a happy home. Reveal yourself to them so that they
may have faith in you. We pray for them to have a right
relationship in you, repenting their sins to one another,
which will bring joy and reconciliation in their families
and finally eternal life. Through Jesus Christ, our Lord.

Miriam Mfitumukiza, Muhabura diocese, Uganda

October 14th – Juana Ines de la Cruz, religious 1695
Father, be near me

Father, be near me:
comfort me when I am distressed;
strengthen me when I am weak;
hold me when I am afraid;
guide me when I am lost.
Laugh with me and share my joy;
sing with me and stir my heart;
fill me up, that I might be renewed
at each day's end, and each day's dawning.
Father, be near me.

Hilary Dale, Lichfield diocese, England

October 15th – Teresa of Avila, mystic and teacher 1582
Hidden handicaps

Lord, we bring before you all who suffer, especially those whose ailments are concealed. Pour out upon them your healing love, we pray, and so strengthen their faith that they may be made whole. Grant to us the grace of consideration, that we be not impatient with uncomprehended handicaps.

   Rochester diocese, England

October 16th – English reformers and martyrs 1555
Prayer for the very ill

Lord, at this moment . . . . . is desperately ill. May they be calmed and comforted by the knowledge that your merciful eyes are watching them. May they get relief during the long, sleepless hours of night and relief from their pain. If it be your will, restore them to health and strength, and comfort all those who watch and wait.

   Brenda Thorpe, York diocese, England

October 17th – Etheldreda, abbess c.639
Healing

Lord, your touch has still its healing power. Here are my hands: take them and use them this day in humble service so that your love may flow through them to someone who needs a human touch.

   Sheila King, Portsmouth diocese, England

October 18th – ST LUKE THE EVANGELIST
For doctors and nurses

Bless, O Lord Christ, all whom you have been called to share in your own ministry of healing as doctors and nurses. Give them skill, understanding and compassion;

and enable them to do their work in dependence on your grace and for the promotion of your glory.

MU Prayer Book, United Kingdom

October 19th – Frideswide, abbess 735
People in hospital

Lord God, whose Son, Jesus Christ, understood people's fear and pain before they spoke of them, we pray for those in hospital. Surround the frightened with your tenderness; give strength to those in pain; hold the weak in your arms of love; and give hope and patience to those who are recovering. We ask this through the same Jesus Christ, our Lord.

Christine McMullen, MU Anthology of Public Prayers, United Kingdom

October 20th – Henry Martyn, missionary 1812
For those who work in clinics and hospitals

Loving Lord Jesus, you spent much of your time on earth healing sick bodies and bringing health to troubled minds. Bless, we pray you, all those who are continuing your work in clinics and hospitals throughout the world. In your name we ask it.

Joyce Care, Llandaff diocese, Wales

October 21st – Hilarion, hermit c.291-371
For the people who work at night

Bless those people, Lord, who stay awake to work whilst we are asleep; the policemen and firemen; those who look after people who are ill; the pilots of planes, the drivers of buses and trains; those whose work we do not know.

Keep them safe from all danger and watch over them in their loneliness; through Jesus Christ, our Lord.

George diocese, South Africa

October 22nd – Philip of Heraclea, bishop and martyr c.304

Healing ministries of this day

O God, we thank you for the gentle healing ministries of this day:
for the gladness and freshness of the morning,
for the freedom of wind and sun,
for the changing beauties of skies and clouds.
We thank you for every remembrance of the past and those who loved you;
for those who have proved steady when all about them was upset;
for those generous in service, whatever the cost to themselves.
For all your many mercies, we give you thanks, O God.

Nan Deedes, Winchester diocese, England

October 23rd – James of Jerusalem, martyr c.62

For strength and courage

God, grant me sympathy and sense,
and strength to hold my courage high.
God, grant me calm and confidence,
and, please, a twinkle in the eye.

Salisbury diocese, England

October 24th – United Nations Day – Raphael, archangel
For the nations of the world

O most Holy Father, iniquities have darkened and made the world sick. But Lord, you said in your word that if your people called by your name call upon you, you will heal their land. We pray that you give us the special grace to humble ourselves, seek your face and turn from our wicked ways, so that you may hear from heaven and heal our nations. In Jesus' name we pray.

Mrs A. O. Tinuoye, Kwara diocese, Nigeria

October 25th – Crispin and Crispinian, martyrs c.285
Prayer for displaced people

Almighty God, our Father, in the name of Jesus I come to you for supplications. You are Immanuel, God with us. You love us all. We know you are not happy when your people are in desperate conditions. The hostilities have made us refugees in our own land. We are without enough clothes, not enough food, and yet our gardens are not cultivated because we left them – we live in camps away from our gardens. One day we are under burning sun; another day under a heavy rain. Our children do not go to school.

O Lord, help us to overcome this situation. O Lord, stop the fighting and resolve the original causes. O Lord, we pray for the restoration of peace in our country so that we may go back to our area to cultivate our gardens to feed our families.

O Lord, we know that you took our nation's sin at the cross. Listen and intervene quickly – many people, especially children and old people, are dying everyday in our camps. Young people are weakened every day. Lord Jesus, look on displaced people's camps. React to their unhygienic conditions.

My Saviour, in you there is hope: you are the Risen Lord; you are the King of Kings; you are the mighty Saviour; you are the Prince of Peace. Come Jesus, come and bring us peace.

A displaced MU member, Rwanda

October 26th – Alfred of Wessex, scholar 899
Prayer of a refugee far from home

O God, our heavenly Father, you are our creator; you separated water from earth, all people are your creatures. God, have mercy upon us: we have sinned against you, we spoiled your creation. We were made to live together but we have been fighting each other. The intelligence you gave us for our betterment people have used for manufacturing guns, bombs and the like; brothers and sisters are killing one another, using them.

Thus, Lord, I ran to another country seeking refuge far from home.

When I wake up in the morning I remember hills and valleys of my country. When shall I go back home, Lord? My children do not have citizenship.

Lord, shall I continue going around countries looking for a better place, looking for facilities, looking for freedom? O Lord, I want to go back to my country to be recognized as a citizen.

O Lord Jesus, you changed my life; I know you can change also my status of being a refugee, being away from my home. I love my country and my people but they do not have confidence in me, so what shall I do?
O Lord, open the gate and I shall go back home. I have all hope in you, Lord.

An MU member who is a refugee in Rwanda

October 27th – Frumentius, bishop 4th century
Thanks for living in a free society

Father, we thank you for the benefits we enjoy by living in a free society: for freedom to worship, for freedom of speech, for freedom of movement. Grant that we may never abuse them nor take them for granted. We pray that the laws of the land are respected, and where they are unjust, to endeavour to get them changed by democratic means.

Portsmouth diocese, England

October 28th – SS. SIMON AND JUDE, APOSTLES
Giving up one's home

O heavenly Father, the time has come for me to give up my home. I am going to live with my children. I thank you for their generosity in receiving me. Help me to accept their love and kindness, not as a right but in gratefulness and love. Help me to be interested in these new surroundings and not to be a burden to those I love.

Chelmsford diocese, England

October 29th – James Hannington and his companions, martyrs 1885
Throughout life

Dear God, thank you for being with me throughout my life. Sometimes I have seen you through people I have met, spoken to, read about. Sometimes I have felt very alone when faced with situations that I haven't understood or known what to do. But somehow things have moved on, sometimes taking a long time – days, weeks, a year. In that time I have felt a sense of strength, occasional sadness and then happiness through the encouragement given to me by those around me.

Please help me to be able to encourage those I meet.
Your life was not easy – you will know and understand
our difficulties even though at times we forget this. Thank
you for your word of hope and the certainty we have of
your love and forgiveness.

Worcester diocese, England

October 30th – Holy women of the New Testament
Go to all nations

O God, your Son commanded us to go to all nations. You
have called us to serve you here in the diocese of . . . . .
Empower us with your Spirit:
give us courage to proclaim Christ crucified;
give us faith to remain firm;
give us a trust to remain ever faithful to you.
Give us a gracious spirit – to extend your kingdom and
righteousness, for Jesus' sake.

St Asaph diocese, Wales

October 31st – Saints and martyrs of the Reformation era
Every day

Remember, O Christian soul, that you have this day and
every day: God to glorify, Jesus to imitate, the Holy Spirit
to recognize, a mind to exercise, a body to hallow,
forgiveness to receive, time to use, neighbours to love,
passions to moderate, gentleness to learn, perfection to
attain, and heaven to hope for.

Salisbury diocese, England

NOVEMBER

Gain and Loss

November 1st – ALL SAINTS
For my godparents

Dear Lord, today I specially remember my godparents.
Bless them and their families, now and always.
   George diocese, South Africa

November 2nd – All Souls
For widows and widowers

O God, our heavenly Father, who does not want us, your
children, to be in sorrow, come down now and be with
our brothers and sisters who have lost their husbands/
wives. Comfort them during their hard times, when they
are alone at night or day; be with them to encourage and
strengthen them. May they pass their days here on earth
in the assurance that they will join you in your heavenly
kingdom where there will be no more sorrow, weeping
and pain.
   Rhoda Ade Olarewaju, Kwara diocese, Nigeria

November 3rd – Martyrs of Mbokotwana
Three generations in the home

Lord, Jesus Christ, you gave your mother into the hands
of your dearest friend. Be with me, I pray, as my father/
mother comes to live with me. Help me to keep the
balance between him/her and my children. Help me to
know when to keep silent, and to do all with love and
understanding. In your name and for your sake.
   Chelmsford diocese, England

November 4th – Martin of Porres, religious 1639
Family life

Dear God, Father of every family, against whom no door can be shut, enter the homes of our land, we pray, with the angel of your presence, that each family may be touched by the beauty of your love.

We open our hearts to you for the families with whom we live day by day. By all that we do or say, help us to build up the faith and confidence of those we love. When we quarrel, help us to forgive quickly.

Help us to welcome new members into our families without reserve, and not to neglect those who in our eyes have become less interesting or more demanding. Abba, dear Father.

Joan Rich, Perth diocese, Australia

November 5th – Cybi, abbot 6th century
Spreading the Good News of life

Lord God, our heavenly Father, set our hearts and minds on fire with the power of your Holy Spirit. Give us courage to respond to your promptings, that we may spread the Good News of life in you and with you, in our own community/church/branch/group. This we ask in Jesus' name.

St Asaph diocese, Wales

November 6th – Leonard, hermit 6th century
For women's groups

O God, we pray for women's groups in our country, which are going ahead for the welfare of the women. We pray especially for . . . . . group/organization/ association, and many others who are aiming to uplift women. Guide their leaders and all the members to fulfil their objectives and so glorify your holy name.

Four women from Kigezi diocese, Uganda

*November 7th – Willibrord, archbishop and missionary
739*
Retirement

Dear Lord, we know that we are all of value to you,
whatever our age. In retirement, teach us to adapt
ourselves to a slower pace of life. Open our eyes to see
that there must be new ways for new times. Show us the
many things we can do with our greater leisure. Help us
to learn more of you as time goes on. Keep us faithful in
prayer and may all our days be lived to your glory.

MU Prayer Book, United Kingdom

November 8th – Saints and martyrs of the British Isles
Give us understanding

Jesus, we come to you to ask for your help in caring for
children. May we show in our lives what following you
means, and so lead them to find you. Give us
understanding when we listen; strength to say the right
words.

Let us not quickly condemn because in our own
childhood life was not the same. Above all, fill our hearts
with your love. Thank you, Lord.

Southwell diocese, England

November 9th – Elisabetta of Dijon, religious 1906
Later life

Lord, now that we are growing older help us to accept
that we cannot rush about as we used to do but have to
take life more easily. Make us realize that we can still do
what you want but in a different way; and that by smiling

and talking kindly to people we are serving you as much
as in the days when we worked more actively. Help us to
remember that now, as in the past, we rest always in you.
  Mrs Evans, Worcester diocese, England

November 10th – Leo the Great, bishop and teacher 461
For the gift of peace

Holy Spirit, give to each of us the precious gift of your
peace. Enable us to bring this peace into all that we think
and do; and strengthen us to work and pray until the
whole world is filled with peace, for Jesus Christ's sake.
  Molly Lucas, Lichfield diocese, England

November 11th – Remembrance Day
Let us be peacemakers

Dear Father in heaven, let us be peacemakers:
more ready to call people friends than enemies,
more ready to trust than to mistrust,
more ready to love than to hate,
more ready to respect than despise,
more ready to serve than be served,
more ready to absorb evil than to pass it on.
Dear Father in heaven, let us be more like Christ.
  MU Anthology of Public Prayers, United Kingdom

November 12th – Tysilio, abbot 6th century
Peace on every creature

Heavenly Father, maker of all things and giver of life, have
mercy on all the nations of the world. Send down your
abundant peace on every creature. Let there be calm
where there is violence; peace where there is war; freedom
where there is bondage; love and unity where there is
strife; abundance of food where there is starvation; good

health where there is sickness; and life where there is death.

These and other good things we ask of you, through our Lord and Saviour, Jesus Christ.

Mrs J. A. Ibimodi, Kwara diocese, Nigeria

November 13th – Charles Simeon, pastor and preacher 1836
Thank you

O Lord, our heavenly Father, the giver of all good gifts, we praise and thank you for all your blessings to us. Forgive us that so often we are more ready to turn to you in times of trouble and need rather than to thank you in the good times. No matter what happens to us, teach us to be thankful. Help us not to take for granted your gift of life itself; our health and strength; the love and support of family and friends; the beauty of your creation. Above all, thank you for your greatest gift – the way of forgiveness you have provided by sending your Son to be our Saviour.

You give us so much, dear Lord. Help us to give you something in return – the love of our hearts, a willingness to serve you and to share your love with others. Grant us day by day a true spirit of thankfulness.

Jean Fenton, Clogher diocese, Ireland

November 14th – Samuel Seabury, bishop 1784
A prayer for our nation and government

O Lord of all creation, bless our nation and government. Let justice be our shield and defender; may we dwell in unity, peace and liberty; let plenty be found within our bodies; let one and all arise for the bright future of our nation.

Let your guidance be our limit. We ask this in the name of Jesus Christ, our Lord.

Four women from Kigezi diocese, Uganda

November 15th – *Helene de Neuville, religious 1904*
For the disabled and the sick

Lord, we thank you for giving us grace. I pray to you to help all these people: disabled, ill, blind, and in all kinds of suffering all over the world. Open their minds to know that you are the creator of everything; if they know you, they will be happy in your kingdom. I pray to turn their sadness into happiness, through Christ, our Lord.

Esther T. John, Yambio diocese, Sudan

November 16th – *Margaret of Scotland, philanthropist 1093*
Prayer of the housebound

Father, thank you for seeing me safely through the night. Keep me happy in the smaller tasks that I can undertake. Thank you for giving me the joy of cheerful visitors.

Gloucester diocese, England

November 17th – *Hugh of Lincoln, bishop 1200*
Prayer of the cared for

Dear Jesus, when I woke up this morning my body ached all over. I felt miserable and low in spirit, trying to cope with the pain and sleeplessness of the night. I asked you, Jesus, to help me through another day. Thank you that once more, Jesus, you heard and answered my prayer.

Monmouth diocese, Wales

November 18th – Hilda of Whitby, abbess 680
Prayer of the carer

Jesus, you know how tired I feel. Give me strength in my body. Let your love and patience be with me, so that I will not speak in a cross voice any words that may hurt. Help us both to love each other as you love us.

Thank you, Jesus, for understanding the needs of us all. Thank you for this day.

June Waters, Monmouth diocese, Wales

November 19th – Elisabeth of Hungary, philanthropist 1231
Afraid of death

God of hope, there are moments when the fear of death sweeps over me like a wave. I'm afraid of life without . . . . . should he/she die first, and I'm afraid of facing my own death.

You are the God of love. Help me to let go all the fears, resentments and hurts I cling to. Help me to trust in you and put my life and . . . . . 's in your hands, in the knowledge that Jesus will be there on the other side waiting for each of us with outstretched arms. In His name I pray.

Joined in Love, New Zealand

November 20th – Edmund of East Anglia, martyr 870
Alone

Lord, I feel so alone – so desolate. Help me draw from you the strength to meet this day's fresh needs. Enable me to make decisions and give me the faith to put the future in your hands. May I find your everlasting joy and understand the purpose of sorrow.

Brenda Thorpe, York diocese, England

November 21st – Gelasius, bishop 5th century
Bereavement

In my grief, numb and empty I come. I come to give the burden I cannot feel; I cannot feel, for to feel is now too much. Too much, for my heart's too full, too full of anger and unshed tears.

Lord, you wept, knew anger and what it is to feel alone. Let my tears spill over to fill the void of loneliness, of being on my own. Help me to remember the good times, link me with those who know this place I'm in.

Empty I come, to be filled with my tears and your love.
Rochester diocese, England

November 22nd – Cecilia, martyr c.230
For those who mourn

Dear God, be with those who mourn and hold their hands, quieten their anger and release their tears. Wrap your loving arms around them and allow them to forgive. Let them accept help and be drawn to your peace. May they hear your still, small voice and be comforted.
Primrose Smith, Southwark diocese, England

November 23rd – Clement of Rome, bishop and martyr c.100
Miscarriages and stillbirths

O God, we pray that you have mercy on women who have had recurrent miscarriages and stillbirths, that your healing miracle might bring joy into such homes. We pray in the name of Jesus Christ, our Lord.
Mrs A. M. Osaji, Kwara diocese, Nigeria

November 24th – Flora and Maria, martyrs 851
Handicapped baby

Dear Lord, I pray for the innocent babies who are handicapped. They may feel out of place, rejected and not wanted, but through friends and adults show them that you really love them, Lord, so that they grow knowing you faithfully. Through Christ, I pray.

Four women from Kigezi diocese, Uganda

November 25th – Elsbeth de Reute, mystic 1420
The new widow

Be with her – when all people have gone.
Be there – through that endless first night alone.
Be there – in those endless nights of fears.
Let her know that you are there, Lord,
showing her your concern and love.
Be there – in the utter loneliness and despair,
when all seems over and nothing matters.
Uphold her – in your love, dear Lord.
Help her to cry out to you for help
so that she may find a sense of purpose
in the future years of her life.
Help her to know you.

Mary Bramley, York diocese, England

November 26th – Sojourner Truth, abolitionist 1883
The gift of our bodies

O Lord, Jesus Christ, we praise you for all the gifts you have given us, especially the parts of our bodies: the mouth to speak, the ears to hear, the brain to think, the hands to catch, the eyes to see, the legs to walk; and especially the Spirit within us, that shall never die. Glory be to God.

Annet Ssemwanga, Bunyoro-Kitara diocese, Uganda

November 27th – Alice Meynell, poet 1922
Advent

Lord of the universe, creator of each one of us,
you became human and weak yet remained God.
Help us in our weaknesses, give us strength,
give us hope until, from the darkness of our sins,
we walk into glory with Christ Jesus.
Eternal God, your purpose will not fail,
your promise will not be broken.
Let your hope take hold of us, now in Advent and for
ever.

*Christine McMullen, MU Anthology of Public Prayers,
United Kingdom*

November 28th – Catherine Labouré, religious 1806-1876
Sharing Christ

Dear Lord, you commanded us to 'go and make disciples'.
Yet, Lord, we often-times have not stopped to ask you
'How?' We are only beginning to consider your command
seriously, and so are daring to ask 'How?'

Make us true disciples, Lord; teach us how to pray
aright; fill us with your Holy Spirit; move us to scripture,
and to fellowship with others so that we may all share in
your resurrection. Help us to find solutions to problems
of sharing our knowledge of you to others, and may all
prepare for your second coming.
In Jesus' name we ask.

Ebun Carr, Gambia diocese, The Gambia

*November 29th – Day of intercession and thanksgiving
for the missionary work of the Church*
Builder of bridges

Make me a builder of bridges, Lord!
Help me to listen more and talk less;
to learn rather than give advice;
to receive when I would rather give;
to acknowledge that I do not have all the truth;
to be rejected, hurt, and humbled;
and ever more deeply to go on loving in Jesus' name.

   Margaret Lawrence, Gloucester diocese, England

November 30th – ST ANDREW THE APOSTLE
Fishermen and sailors

Heavenly Father, defend all fishermen and sailors in every
peril of the deep, and grant your blessing to all those who
seek to bring them succour and support.

   Joyce Care, Llandaff diocese, Wales

DECEMBER

Anticipation

December 1st – Charles de Foucauld 1916
Advent

Lord, as we approach the season of Advent make us
watchful and heedful in awaiting the coming of your Son,
Jesus Christ; that when He shall come and knock, He
shall not find us sleeping.

We pray for all who are lonely and afraid, and for those
for whom the coming season of Christmas is a time to be
endured but not enjoyed.

May we all be willing and ready to play our part in
whatever you call us to do, however small. We humbly
pray that you bless adundantly the preparations now
being made for your coming. Prepare all hearts to receive
your word and grant that it may take deep root and bring
forth fruit in due season. O Lord, hear our prayer.

Nan Deedes, Winchester diocese, England

*December 2nd – Nicholas Ferrar, deacon and religious
1637*
A Bible study group

O God, our Father, you reveal yourself to us through the
scriptures. Let your Holy Spirit open our hearts and minds
to your word that together we may grow in faith and love
and witness to you in our homes and in your world.

This we ask of you through your Son, Christ, our Lord.
Norwich diocese, England

December 3rd – Saints and martyrs of Asia
This day

Lord Jesus Christ, you have given me this day to live for
you. May I know you and your purpose for me, your
presence with me, your power in me, all day.

Cicely Jenkins, Southwark diocese, England

December 4th – Clement of Alexandria, theologian c.217
God will not fail us

Dear Lord, please help us to honour you in all that we do, think and say today. Help us to live for you that others may see you in our lives and glorify your name.

Lord, when we think you are failing us, help us to know that you are not capable of failing and that you are always ready to hear our prayers and to help us in time of need. Thank you for restoring the fortunes of your people.

Have mercy on us, O God. Wash us thoroughly from our iniquity and cleanse us from our sins.

East Ankole diocese, Uganda

December 5th – Peter Masiza, priest 1907
Bedtime prayer

. O everliving God, we thank you for your fatherly care; thank you for our daily bread; thank you for making the world so sweet and comfortable to live in. Thank you, God, for bringing us to see the end of another day.

In the name of our Lord and Saviour, Jesus Christ, forgive us all our sins which we have committed today in thought, word and deed. Grant us a happy and peaceful rest; protect us from the snares and perils of this night; help us to overpower all our enemies that will arise against us in dreams this night.

Our Father, give us sound sleep and when it is daybreak may we rise up with good health and peace to glorify your holy name.

In Jesus Christ's name I pray.

Hannah Haruna J.P., Kwara diocese, Nigeria

December 6th – Nicholas, bishop c.342
Each child is special

Creator God, you made us all in your image and yet each of us is different and each has infinite value in your sight.

May we treasure our children as individuals in their own right. They have different skills, different personalities, different temperaments. Guide us as we nurture their skills, develop their personalities, understand their temperaments; that each may be whole, able to stand on their own, strong in a living faith in the God who created them.

Joined in Love, New Zealand

December 7th – Ambrose, bishop and teacher 397
Your image in others

Lord God, help us to see your image in others, that we may learn to love those whom we find it hard to like.

Barbara Saunders, Portsmouth diocese, England

December 8th – Richard Baxter, theologian 1691
Your image in us

Lord Jesus Christ, we thank you that you came to earth, not to be served but to serve, and to give your life as a ransom for us all. Give us your light, we pray, and help us to follow your example and to walk in your footsteps, that we may look for opportunities to show the reality of our faith in serving others so that they may see your image in us, and give glory to your name.

Coventry diocese, England

December 9th – Holy men of the Old Testament
The Bible

We thank you, heavenly Father, that you have spoken to your people through the Bible, your written word. We thank you that you have spoken to us through your Son, Jesus Christ. Make us willing to give time and concentration to study your word, and give us quietness of mind and heart to hear you speak to us by your Spirit.

Chester diocese, England

December 10th – Thomas Merton, monk and writer 1968
Thanks

May our God be glorified and always be given thanks for listening to us.

Josephine Rwaje, Byumba diocese, Rwanda

December 11th – Octavius Hadfield, bishop 1904
A prayer for transport

I pray for some parts in our country, ..., where there are no good roads and transport. Many people in these places when they are sick, they die without being treated. We pray to you, our creator and provider, to look on your people and find a way of succouring them. I believe that to you nothing is impossible. Hear my prayer through our Saviour, Jesus Christ.

Bunyoro–Kitara diocese, Uganda

December 12th – Jane Frances de Chantal, abbess 1641
Prayer for those working for the Government

Heavenly Father, you created us to be your people and you gave us different minds to have different jobs. I pray to you this day to lead all the people working in the Government; send them your Holy Spirit that all they do to others may be in your love, so that your name may be praised.

Hellen Ngbagida, Yambio diocese, Sudan

December 13th – Lucy of Syracuse, martyr c.304
The worldwide Church

O God, our Father, bless your Church with unity, peace and concord. Make her here and all over the world a true fellowship of the Spirit, in which no distinction is made because of race, colour, class or party; a fellowship of love in which all are really in Christ.

We ask it in His name, who is our one Lord.
Birmingham diocese, England

December 14th – John of the Cross, teacher and mystic 1591
Give us this day our daily bread

Heavenly Father, look mercifully upon those who have no work to earn their daily bread, and cannot use the gifts and abilities that you have given them. We pray for them and their families and ask that relief and help will come to them. In your mercy, strengthen the faith of those who know you and give faith to those who do not.

Bless the efforts of those who strive to alleviate their suffering, and show us how to be sensitive and helpful to those around us.

Father, forgive us and send us all patience and trust in our Saviour, Jesus Christ, through whom we pray.
Edna Wilson, Oxford diocese, England

December 15th – Maria di Rosa, religious 1855
The kingdom of heaven is like a mustard seed

In arid wastes a child's eyes plead,
feed my need.
Will the silent child recall whose bread
fed when he is grown? No, never known.
It is enough to take his hand
that he may stand.
  Rochester diocese, England

December 16th – Marianne Williams, missionary 1879
Help

Dear heavenly Father, thank you for the nice things we get
each day which keep us in comfort. Help those who
haven't got these things. Help us to be kind and generous.
  Rosalind (aged 11), Chelmsford diocese, England

December 17th – Olympias, deaconess c.410
Prayer for noisy neighbours

O Lord, our heavenly Father, into your hands we
commend our neighbours, who have no thought of
bringing souls to you but bring hatred between
neighbours in the community. Help them to love and give
respect and service to neighbours, as you have said, 'Love
your neighbour as yourself.'
  Lord, in your mercy, hear our prayer.
  Bo diocese, Sierra Leone

December 18th – Dorothy Sayers, author 1957
For grandchildren, nieces, nephews and godchildren

Almighty God, Father of our Lord, Jesus Christ, we bring
our grandchildren, nieces, nephews and godchildren to
you. Let us train them in your way as Lois, Timothy's

grandmother, brought him up. Her good deeds could never be forgotten and have become examples to subsequent generations. Make us good examples to them. Help us never to mislead them by our words and actions, through the help of Jesus Christ, the Good Teacher.

Rhoda Ade Olarewaju, Kwara diocese, Nigeria

December 19th – Holy children of the Old Testament
The homeless

O Father, I live here in this lovely home – warm, comfortable and fed – aware of those sleeping rough this night in cardboard city. What can I do? Even if I gave everything up the problem would not go away. Father, move our hearts that we may do what we can: give; lobby our Members of Parliament; and commit the suffering to you, who entered into the suffering of man.

Thank you, Father, for being there now with the occupant of the cardboard box.

Beryl Denney, Chelmsford diocese, England

December 20th – Ignatius of Antioch, bishop and martyr c.107
For refugees

Lord, our heavenly Father, who out of your love for mankind sent your dear Son, Jesus Christ, to leave His heavenly glory and come to redeem us; we thank you, Father, because He has revealed you as the light of the world. Through Him men are able to see and recognize each other as brothers or sisters even when they may have differences.

We pray, Lord, that this light may shine in our hearts so that we may be able to live as brothers and sisters and have concern for one another. We pray particularly for the refugees, the hungry, and the suffering communities in some countries of the world.

Lord, in your mercy, shine in the selfish heart of man so that our leaders may be guided by that light to bring about peace, harmony and reconciliation in their countries. We thank you for those who are concerned with relief for the refugees. We pray this through Jesus Christ, our Lord.

Joy Shalita, Muhabura diocese, Uganda

December 21st – Juliana of Smolensk, martyr c.1406
For my family

Thank you, Lord, for my family who love me. Help me to be loving too, and to show them that I care. Bless us all . . . . . and keep us in your care.

George diocese, South Africa

December 22nd – Jutta of Diessenberg, teacher 1136
Prayer for a safe delivery

Most heavenly Father of the human race behold me, unworthy though I am; see that I am about to have a baby. I pray that you assist me to bear the pain of childbirth courageously, and give me physical and moral strength. Avert from me any unseen or unnatural circumstance and grant me the privilege of bearing a normal, healthy baby. Hear my humble prayer, dear Lord, offered to you with confidence and love in this hour of my expectation. Help me to be a good mother in word and example. Grant that after my delivery my little baby may learn at an early age of your greatness. May the joy and peace of a safe delivery fill my heart, and may your blessed name be praised now and for evermore.

Sister E. Gbonda, Bo diocese, Sierra Leone

December 23rd – Anysia, benefactor c.304
Please make each heart a manger

Dear God, we will be very busy again this Christmastime, and we know that we will be tempted to forget the true meaning of this festival. Please help us to conquer these temptations, so that we may share with our families the true joy of our Saviour's birth. Lord, we have sung our Christmas carols and heard the Nativity story so many times before; help us, in our acts of worship to recapture the wonder of this glad season. Please make each heart a manger and each home a Bethlehem. We pray this in the name of Jesus Christ, our Saviour.

Edith Williams, Monmouth diocese, Wales

December 24th – Christmas Eve
Christmas Eve

He wasn't rich or posh. He had no stocking,
no presents, turkey, mince pies. It was shocking.
He had no cot, no baby-gro or rattle
but just a bed of straw among the cattle.

So, as we spoil ourselves and one another
(I've even got a present for my brother),
tomorrow in our hearts let's hold and keep
a picture of that baby fast asleep.

God's Christmas gift to us – yes, everyone –
Himself: His love revealed through Christ, His Son.
With all our other presents, Lord, please may
we give ourselves, give love this Christmas Day.

Kate (aged 8) and her mother, Joanna Durham-Matthews, Winchester diocese, England

December 25th – Christmas Day
Keeping Christ in Christmas

Thank you, God, for the wonderful gift of your Son, Jesus, as we celebrate His birthday. Help us to remember Him as we give and receive gifts, taking time to pray for each person and for those who have nothing.

Thank you for the Christmas tree, a wonderful symbol of your glorious creation. Please help us to care for it.

Thank you for the lights on the tree, reminding us of Jesus, the Light of the world, and of how we too must shine for Him.

Thank you for gaiety and feasting; may it be in your honour, Jesus.

Help us, Lord, to fill this Christmas with you and with your love, peace and joy.

Marjorie Hodbod, Blackburn diocese, England

December 26th – ST STEPHEN THE FIRST MARTYR
Giving and receiving

Lord, help us to give ourselves when we are giving presents.

Teach us to give without thought of receiving and to receive without thought of giving.

Teach us not to withhold or withdraw ourselves.

Teach us to hoard nothing – love, money, time, possessions.

Teach us to give even our life if required of us, and while we have it, to use it as an instrument of your peace.

Christine McMullen, MU Anthology of Public Prayers, United Kingdom

December 27th – ST JOHN THE EVANGELIST
The candle

Look at the candle and the flame that comes from it –
sometimes flickering, sometimes burning steadily,
sometimes with black smoke rising and disappearing into
the air.

Our hearts are as the wick within the candle – we are
that wick. God is the flame that ignites us so that we
shine out into the darkness. The black smoke that we
sometimes see is the fire of God, burning and refining us,
removing the things that stand between God and us.

Round the wick is the tallow of the candle – this stands
for God's love: enclosing, encircling, and giving the fuel
for the wick to burn in a steady light. If we are the wick
then it is up to us what kind of flame we show – a
flickering, dying flame; or a strong vigorous flame that
has God's light shining through, and one that is prepared
to let the black smoke rise as we allow God to purify us.

Christ is our light, our flame. Let us take Him into the
wick of our hearts and let His light blaze through as
brightly as the lights on a Christmas tree, so that all can
see that we are alight with the love of Christ.

Rochester diocese, England

December 28th – THE HOLY INNOCENTS
Death of a child

Father of all, stretch out your loving arms to the mother
and father who mourn their child, ... Draw them gently
to you in their grief; comfort them in the emptiness that is
left, and give them strength and courage to face the future.

Lord, give us understanding and compassion to say the
right words and be sensitive to their needs.

Eunice Davies, St Albans diocese, England

December 29th – Thomas Becket, archbishop and martyr 1170

Accidents

Father of all goodness, the creator of heaven and earth, we plead with you to keep us from all kinds of accidents and calamities. Give us your sound security and full protection that we may be able to move in, out and about without fear or regret.

Grant those who have sustained injury in one accident or the other quick recovery. For these we ask, through Jesus Christ, our Lord.

Mrs V. B. Okunrintemi, Kwara diocese, Nigeria

December 30th – Josephine Butler, social reformer 1906

For social workers and voluntary agencies

We thank you, O God, for those who work in the Social Services and voluntary agencies in our country and in our own community. Be with them in their efforts to mend broken lives and broken homes; to help the alcoholic and drug addict; to minister to people in despair.

Encourage them, dear Lord, when the tasks seem overwhelming; give them wisdom when situations seem insoluble; and give them in their work all needful patience, sympathy and understanding. This we ask in the name of Jesus Christ, our Saviour.

Nan Deedes, Winchester diocese, England

December 31st – John Wyclif, theologian and reformer 1384

A journey

O God, you gave me life, free will and a conscience and set me out on a journey like a pilgrim, a journey with many turnings and signposts.

Sometimes I've strayed, but with prayer and meditation I've returned to you with peace in my heart.

I pray that at the end of my journey I will pass from the dark to the light, and in the company of your saints give praise and glory to your name.

Carlisle diocese, England

Appendix

The Mothers' Union Wave of Prayer

O God, our heavenly Father, we ask you to bless the work of the Mothers' Union throughout the world, and especially in each diocese for which we pray today. Bless our members in their lives and in their homes, that they, being strengthened in love to you and to each other, may serve you faithfully to your glory, through Jesus Christ, our Lord, Amen.

January 1st to 5th
Lesotho, Bermuda, Cyangugu, Canterbury

January 6th to 10th
Enugu, On the Niger, Awka, Gambia, York

January 11th to 15th
Bo, Freetown, Mandalay, Myitkyina, London

January 16th to 20th
Ruwenzori, S Ruwenzori, Bunyoro-Kitara, Durham

January 21st to 25th
Masasi, Algoma, Muhabura, Winchester

January 26th to 31st
Matabeleland, Katsina, Bangor

February 1st to 5th
Lebombo, Niassa, Kampala, Bath and Wells

February 6th to 10th
Natal, Mityana, Oke Osun, Birmingham

February 11th to 15th
Bloemfontein, Sekondi/Takoradi, Shyogwe, Blackburn

February 16th to 20th
St John's, Busoga, Umzimvubu, Bradford

February 21st to 25th
Johannesburg, Klerksdorp, West Ankole, Bristol

February 26th to 29th
The staff and work of Mary Sumner House

March 1st to 5th
Zululand, Swaziland, Women in North Argentina,
    Carlisle

March 6th to 10th
George, Hpa'an, Taungoo, Members in Thailand,
    Chelmsford

March 11th to 15th
Cape Town, Namibia, Mbaise, Chester

March 16th to 20th
Kimberley and Kuruman, Owo, Chichester

March 21st to 25th
Central Zambia, Toamasina, Antananarivo, Coventry

March 26th to 31st
Central Overseas Committee, All Diocesan Overseas
    Chairmen and Links Correspondents

April 1st to 5th
Juba, Yambio, Kajo-Keji, Maridi, Yei, Kigali, Shyira,
    Byumba, Ely

April 6th to 10th
Vanuatu, Temotu, Antsiranana, Exeter

April 11th to 15th
Popondota, Bukavu, Ondo, Ekiti, Gloucester

April 16th to 20th
Lahore, Asaba, Jos, Makurdi, Yola, Guildford

April 21st to 25th
Mara, Members in North India, Hereford

April 26th to 30th
Mt Kilimanjaro, Port Moresby, Botswana, Leicester

May 1st to 5th
Central Melanesia, Hanuato'o, Ysabel, Malaita,
  Sunyani/Tamale, Lichfield

May 6th to 10th
Dhaka, Women's Fellowship in South India, Kano,
  Maiduguri, Bauchi, Lincoln

May 11th to 15th
Sittway, Yangon, Warri, Benin, Sabongidda-Ora,
  Liverpool

May 16th to 20th
Kwara, Koforidua, Katakwa, Llandaff

May 21st to 25th
Maseno South, Masono West, Sabah, North Kivu,
  Manchester

May 26th to 31st
Harare, SE Transvaal, Kushdia, Monmouth

June 1st to 5th
Zanzibar and Tanga, Dar-es-Salaam, Polynesia, Newcastle

June 6th to 10th
Ibadan, Osun, Ife, Guyana, Aipo Rongo, New Guinea Is.,
  Norwich

June 11th to 15th
Owerri, Okigwe-Orlu, Kisangani, Boga-Zaire, Oxford

June 16th to 20th
Pusan, Seoul, Taejon, Manicaland, Peterborough

June 21st to 25th
Sydney, Lagos, Remo, Egba-Abeokuta, Egbado, Portsmouth

June 26th to 30th
Bathurst, Namirembe, Mukono, Luwero, Ripon

July 1st to 5th
Canberra and Goulburn, Lake Malawi, South Malawi,
    Rochester

July 6th to 10th
Armidale, Grafton, Lusaka, Christ the King, Akoko, St
    Albans

July 11th to 15th
Newcastle (Aus.), Riverina, Mbale, Bukedi, North Mbale,
    St Asaph

July 16th to 20th
Melbourne, Wangaratta, Grahamstown, St David's

July 21st to 25th
Ballarat, Kirinyaga, Mt Kenya Central, Mt Kenya South,
    Mt Kenya West, Windward Is., St Edmundsbury and
    Ipswich

26th to 31st July
Bendigo, Gippsland, Nakuru, Rumbek, Khartoum, Bor,
    Wau, Mundri, Khadugli, Salisbury

August 1st to 5th
Brisbane, West Buganda, Maseno North, Nambale,
    Sheffield

August 6th to 10th
Rockhampton, Trinidad and Tobago, Akure, Sodor and Man

August 11th to 15th
Niger Delta, Aba, Calabar, Uyo, Carpentaria, Northern
    Territory, Southwark

August 16th to 20th
Dogura, North Queensland, Victoria Nyanza, Kagera,
    Southwell

August 21st to 25th
Perth, Bunbury, Mobasa, Nairobi, Machakos, Swansea
  and Brecon

August 26th to 31st
Nelson, Barbados, Shaba, Truro

September 1st to 5th
Adelaide, The Murray, Willochra, Soroti, Karamoja,
  Wakefield

September 6th to 10th
NW Australia, East Ankole, Kigezi, North Kigezi, Minna,
  Worcester

September 11th to 15th
The Lundi, Tasmania, Ottawa, Armagh

September 16th to 20th
Christchurch, Kumasi, Accra, West Tanganyika, Tabora,
  Dublin and Glendalough

September 21st to 25th
Auckland, Waikato, Central Tanganyika, Morogoro,
  Ruaha, Meath and Kildare

September 26th to 30th
Wellington, Ilesa, Cape Coast, Clogher

October 1st to 5th
Nova Scotia, Fredericton, Madi and West Nile, North
  Uganda, Lango, Derry and Raphoe

October 6th to 10th
Montreal, Dunedin, Belize, Connor

October 11th to 15th
Mauritius, Seychelles, Kajiado, Kilmore

October 16th to 20th
Butare, Port Elizabeth, Embu, Kigeme, Derby

October 21st to 25th
Ijebu, Niagara, Calgary and Edmonton, Waiapu, Cashel
   and Ossory

October 26th to 31st
Rupert's Land, Eldoret, Kaduna, Abuja, Kafanchan, Cork

November 1st to 5th
Central Lone and Indoor Members Worldwide

November 6th to 10th
The Central President, Dominion and Provincial Presidents

November 11th to 15th
Prince Edward Island, Saskatoon, Buye, Bujumbura,
   Matana, Tuam

November 16th to 20th
Toronto, Pretoria, St Mark the Evangelist, Gitega, Down
   and Dromore

November 21st to 25th
New Westminster, Kootenay, SW Tanganyika, Ruvuma,
   Aberdeen

November 26th to 30th
Colombo, Kurunagala, Mpwapwa, Edinburgh

December 1st to 5th
NE Caribbean and Aruba, Rift Valley, Glasgow and
   Galloway

December 6th to 10th
Jamaica, Sokoto, St Andrews, Dunkeld and Dunblane

December 11th to 15th
British Columbia, Qu'Appelle, North Zambia, Limerick
   and Killaloe

December 16th to 20th
Provincial Trainers, Provincial Workers, Community
   Workers

December 21st to 25th
Jerusalem and the Middle East

December 26th to 31st
Families throughout the world

Thematic Index

Foster children	May 15
Godchildren	May 19, Dec 18
Godparents	Nov 1
Going astray	Aug 20
Grandchildren	May 19, Jul 26, Dec 18
Growing up	Feb 19, May 21, Oct 8
Help us	Feb 20
Home	Feb 5
Leaving school	Jul 19
Little children	May 3
Lost son	Aug 27
New school	Jan 31
Nieces and nephews	Dec 18
Orphans	Feb 12
Out into the world	May 24
Playgroup helpers	Feb 24
Pram service	May 2
Relationships	Aug 16
Safety	Feb 25
Schoolchildren	May 11
Senior schools	Sep 13
Son in armed forces	Apr 8
Starting school	Sep 12
Starving	Dec 15
Taking exams	Aug 17
Teenagers	Aug 18
Too many girls	Feb 17
Understanding	Nov 8
Understanding others	May 25
Without parents	May 7
Young people	Aug 22

Church's Year	
Advent	Nov 27, Dec 1
Ascension	May 20
Candlemas	Feb 2
Christmas Day	Dec 25
Christmas Eve	Dec 24
Easter	Apr 14
Epiphany	Jan 6

Marriage

Battered wife	Jul 14
Continuing	Jul 13
Daughters-in-law	Oct 12
Early days	Feb 15
For husbands	Jul 8
Growing together	Feb 26
Husband's prayer	Mar 19
In-laws	Apr 20
Married children	Oct 11
Mixed marriage	Oct 10
Nagging wives	Jul 9
Not sharing faith	Jul 7
Polygamous homes	Apr 22
Relationships	Aug 16
Second marriage	Apr 21
Sons-in-law	Oct 12
Strengthening	Apr 19
Time to enjoy	Aug 7
Wedding day	Apr 18

Medical

Clinic/hospital work	Oct 20
Doctors and nurses	Oct 18
Midwives and nurses	Jan 11

Ministry

Builder of bridges	Nov 29
Carer	Nov 18
Channels of joy	Apr 30
Church cleaners	Jun 20
Church work	May 9
Clergy	Sep 30
Concern for neighbours	Aug 14
Dare to give	Apr 7
Doing	Mar 11
Flower arrangers	Jun 17
For each other	Apr 10
For others	Mar 12
Generous help	Jul 29
Giving and receiving	Dec 26